Southern As I See It

A Practical Guide to Manners, Traditions,
and
Things Your Mama Shoulda Taught You

By

Alcinda Chandler Smith

*Lynn Jones,
I know your
mama raised
you right!
Cindy Smith*

Delta Girl Publishing

Southern As I See It
A Practical Guide to Manners, Traditions,
And
Things Your Mama Shoulda Taught You

By
Alcinda Chandler Smith

Published by
Delta Girl Publishing
Copyright © Alcinda Chandler Smith, 2020

ISBN: 978-0-578-78170-9

Cover design by
Merritt Haddock

Printed in the United States of America

Publisher's Note:
While the author has made every effort to provide accurate telephone numbers, Internet addresses, and other contact information at the time of publication, neither the publisher nor the author assumes any responsibility for errors, or for changes that occur after publication.

Printed in the United States of America
Library of Congress Cataloging-in-Publications data
Chandler Smith, Alcinda, 1959-

<u>Dedication</u>

To all the people who made me a better person. Whether you corrected me, encouraged me, laughed with me, or just loved me, you made this book come to life.

To my husband and children. You are my pride and joy.

To my best friends. You know who you are if you have ever piled up in the bed with me on a lazy day. (Or if I drank your fine wine and later threw up in your fountain.)

TABLE OF CONTENTS

Introduction

When I was in the fourth grade, my Grandma Dorsel gave me my first etiquette book, *White Gloves and Party Manners.* My grandparents lived in an elegant apartment in the Watergate in Washington, D.C. Yes, the same place made famous by the scandal. There were pictures of Grampa Toby and her in formalwear on a shelf by their baby grand piano. When I visited them, we would dress up and attend performances at the Kennedy Center for Performing Arts, just next door. I was the first girl born into the Chandler family in 84 years, so needless to say, I was a little spoiled. Thus, began my love of fine things and formal affairs. I've been perusing etiquette books ever since.

Disclaimer

Despite this seemingly prestigious upbringing, I'm just a regular gal. I pretty much have a potty mouth. I've been known to enjoy a little gossip, and I was called into Standards once (my sorority's governing body) for staying out all night while in college.

I'm somewhat of an interrupter. In fact, I've been (lovingly?) called a "blurter" by some of my best friends. I eat casual meals with my elbows on the table. Punctuality is not my strong suit. It's not that I have never committed a faux pas (I have...many), but I try to do better, or at least know what is correct. I like to laugh, and you should, too.

Please give me some slack. I don't feel it, but apparently, I'm old. When I fill in my birth date in an online application, I have to spin that wheel like I'm on *The Price is Right* to get down to 1959. And, when I was growing up, *thongs* were *flip flops*. The smallest panties I've ever worn were hip-huggers.

I have to turn down the radio in the car, when it's raining hard, so I can concentrate better. And I can't hear when I can't find my glasses.

And, I ugly cry. I look horrible, when skiing and take off my hat in the lodge. I'm in awe of those ladies who simply shake their heads and look freshly coifed.

So, try to like me, okay?

I'm assuming you bought this book to learn and/or confirm what is considered correct in the South. I don't want to be held responsible for "The Rules" everywhere, just down here, y'all.

I moved to the South when I was 16. Until that time, I lived first in Minnesota; then "out west." I'm grateful that people I meet now just assume I'm Southern. A certain kindness and hospitality is associated with Southerners, so I take pride in the association. I suppose *graciousness* is what it is.

It's not my fault I wasn't born here, but I thank God everyday that this is where I ended up. I try to be as Southern as possible, and have enjoyed learning and preserving Southern etiquette since I arrived south of the Mason-Dixon line. We like people to know we're Southern. It's obvious from our accents, but we consider it **braggin' rights**.

After all, no one wants to be called a *Yankee*.

This book needed to be written. Actually, it probably should have been written ten years ago, to prevent the complete fall of Southern society. People "not from the South" don't understand our desire to be kind and put others at ease. My wish is to put to paper some thoughts about the correct way to present oneself, while expressing my sincere gratitude for living in the South.

My intent when considering this book was to show Southern graciousness, Southern pride, and the Southern way of **doin' thangs**. Customs and protocol abound, but for many traditions born in the South, is a desire for preservation. For the purpose of exhibiting my love of all things Southern, I will capitalize the S in the word. Enjoy.

Cindy Smith is writing a book about etiquette? In writing the book, my friends all said, "Great, I'll need several copies." But I always felt like they were silently saying, "~~What the Hell?~~ Cindy? What does she know?"

My Youth

Early in life, the last thing you want is to be like your mama. But believe me, as you get older and raise your own children you will hear her in yourself. At first you will be stunned, ~~then mortified~~, and later you will be honored to be compared to her.

My Mother knew the rules. Joyce Ann was a preacher's kid. She and her brothers grew up eating supper by candlelight. The Methodist ladies gave my Grandmère the "too short to continue to burn during worship" candles from the altar, so she put them to good use. Mom carried this legacy to our dinner table, and most of our evening meals were in the dining room, seated at a candlelit table. My brothers and I naturally played the game of running our fingers through the flame, but at least we were exposed to the essential need for decorum at the table.

She taught us to pass the salt WITH the pepper. She taught us to pass the salad, vegetables, butter, etc. to our neighbor to the RIGHT, until everyone was served, BEFORE we started eating. She taught us to take the breadbasket and remove a roll, instead of grabbing a roll out of an extended basket. (We learned this quickly, because she would drop the basket if we forgot!) We also knew to put butter on our butter plates and tear our bread into pieces, buttering each piece just before eating it. (This keeps crumbs off the butter and is polite.) If you pick up the breadbasket, it is correct to ask the person to your right and to your left before serving yourself. She served "family style" which is a lot more work than serving directly from the kitchen.

My parents (Dad, Bill, a paper mill engineer, and early computer geek) began the meal with prayer, something we all became familiar with and grateful for. We had dessert with every evening meal. We had lively family discussions. We spilled some milk. We stopped conversations to look up words in the dictionary. We used cloth napkins.

Grandmère, my mother's mother, had a beautiful home near the D.C. neighborhood of Georgetown, with huge trees and beautiful flowers, and a "morning room" where she did her sewing with the sun shining in the windows. She was a proud member of the Daughters of the American Revolution, traveled the world, and all her meals were served on china in her dining room. I remember these things, so I don't mind when my grandchildren play with her silver tea service on my dining room floor. In fact, it makes me happy. My grandfather, a chaplain, baptized me as a toddler. He passed away not long afterwards, but isn't that special?

My "Watergate" grandparents had an interesting life. They worked together in their business, The Film Center, where they rented movie projectors and films to businesses and even to the Presidents' wives, for entertaining in the White House. They had a weekend home on Chesapeake Bay. My brothers and I have memories of the Bay House, crabbin' in the evenings and inviting local kids to watch movies on the side porch after dark.

Growing up with my brothers, our family wasn't always formal. We sometimes got to eat hamburgers on Friday evenings, from trays in front of the TV. This was a huge deal. So was going to A&W for root beer floats. The waitress hooked that tray to the car window and I wished I could be her with that change thingy on her belt. I even remember going to McDonald's after church occasionally, back when their burgers were only a quarter, and a medium sized drink was only 12 oz., not today's 30. No wonder America battles being fat obesity.

In the 60s, TV dinners were new and popular, but my mom never fell for that. Oh, how I wanted to eat that little mound of instant mashed potatoes from an aluminum tray. She did let us have Jiffy-Pop Popcorn, though... and Fizzies. And we even thought Tang was delicious. (You know, the astronauts drank Tang!) That was back in the time of candy cigarettes.

My father arrived home each evening at 5:30 and read his mail until one of us got to ring the dinner bell. It was just a little brass bell, but an honor to whomever got the job. Then we all sat down together. I know.... together, with no cell phones at the table. Kinda hard to imagine, now.

I married a farmer (Don, but since his 40th birthday, we all call him Daddy Don.) My son, Taylor, was an athlete that made this mama's heart proud. (Daughter, Natalie, will be introduced soon.) Looking back, it seems like my children mostly ate from the concession stand at the baseball field. When Don would arrive for the game, I would give him some popcorn, and say, "Your appetizer, Sir."

When we did eat at home, we fought over the one chair at the kitchen counter, usually eating a couple of hours before Don even got in from the fields. We have both a breakfast room table, and a lovely dining room, but standing in the kitchen just gave us more time to visit. We ate as a family when we had the opportunity, and we have some good memories of those supper table discussions. Presumably, I taught my children good table manners, as I'm not embarrassed to watch them eat today. Taylor likes to tell the story of me chasing him upstairs because he wouldn't try creamed corn (The child could gag at will) — and when I caught him on the landing he was **hollerin'**, "She's killin' me!"

Yes, I believe in discipline.

One of the first things I loved when I moved to the South was how waitresses and hairdressers called me **darlin'**. I find that to be so sweet, and kind. Now, "honey" can mean different things, but not "darlin'." And using the word "darlin," really helps if you are unable to remember someone's name.

What else do I love about the South? A Southerner's initial reaction is to smile and extend kindness. We gently nod our heads and lift our index finger from the steering wheel when we meet another car on the street. We let other drivers go ahead of us, and appreciate the "courtesy wave."

We take food to those in need.

Have you ever been to Charlotte, North Carolina? Y'all, they have rocking chairs in the airport just to make you feel welcomed.

I think good manners and civility are bred into a Southern woman's nature. They hesitate, and then decide to say or do something nice. Some call it Southern charm.

Southern women embrace femininity, and are nurturing, strong, and self-assured.

We are independent. We are not shrinking violets. We are capable of taking care of ourselves. And some are tomboys. Many like to hunt, and we sure like working in the garden.

Southern women don't have to be feminists. We've been in control all along. We value men and let them help us as a kindness to them, not a weakness on our part. But I do appreciate all who came before me to aid in achieving equality.

I have never changed a tire. I don't mind asking any random man in Lowe's where to find what I'm looking for. (Since I can never find an employee when I need one!) We don't think a man helping us makes us appear helpless. I believe men enjoy being needed and appreciated. **Bless their hearts**.

I've sanded and stained, hauled mulch, and planted truckloads of flowers and shrubs. I can obviously change a light bulb. I think I can boost a car and replace the net on a basketball goal. But why? The only time a Southern woman is really helpless is when her fingernail polish is still wet. (I read that somewhere... wish it were original.)

We are not submissive, uneducated, or without goals. When the word *domestic* is used, it means we love our homes. We enjoy entertaining and preparing a special meal. It doesn't mean we put on an apron every morning and wait on others all day. Although, if we did, it would be our loved ones, and that's all right, too.

We say *please* and *thank you* without reservation. We teach our children to say *Ma'am* and *Sir* out of respect, and as adults we continue this tradition with our elders. Yankees often mistake the sir/ma'am thing for sassiness. It truly is meant to show respect and kindness. Sometimes, though, this **good trainin'** can go too far. Once, after getting a speeding ticket, I thanked the highway patrolman. Then I laughed and told him I needed to take that back, but to have a nice day.

Southern women of today aren't brought up to settle down and find a husband and raise a family — that whole MRS Degree went out with girdles and nylons — that's what I **chose**. And I chose for love and I chose well. I thank God for that. In no way do I want the reader to think a Southern lady is under the spell of a mother who directs her every move and expects her to be submissive. I am a college graduate who moved to a small town to marry the man she loved.

Our daughter, Natalie, is married to a wonderful man (Josh) — her high school sweetheart. And she is intelligent, beautiful, feminine, and quite successful. They manage to balance work with love of family. They made us grandparents of precious boy/girl twins. They love their church, and she loves her in-laws. They make us proud every day. She's her own woman and I am grateful we are close.

Another thing I love about the South is that we Southerners are sociable. We just like to visit. We strike up conversations with total strangers. I don't hesitate to ask people if they will share a table. I don't mind holding a person's place in line. What is to be gained by being impatient or rude? (But I have zero patience for someone who cuts in line).

The South is a region, but it is moreover a state of mind.

Part One
Rules to get us started

Why Me?

I owned a gift shop for 27 years and printed stationery as well. People came to depend on me to tell them what was "right." Whether it was questions about wedding or baby registries, what name to put on a notecard, or what time constitutes "brunch" on an invitation. (It's 9 to 2, by the way, but bellinis, Bloody Marys, and mimosas shouldn't come out until 11.)

While waiting on my customers, I earned the reputation of being someone to ask about **doin' things**. Oftentimes I'd call my mother, or any of the many women I respected in my church family who would know the answer. I was asked endless ~~silly~~ questions, but I genuinely wanted to help and be correct. I guess that's what ultimately led me to consider writing this. I remember in the '80s reading *Miss Manners' Guide to Excruciatingly Correct Behavior.* I was stunned so many people had questions. My Mom was always present in my childhood to gently guide me. When I started thinking about the ridiculous things I've seen, I thought it prudent to document for posterity some things I've learned.

I know etiquette is constantly reinterpreted and changing. But everyone needs a starting point.

So, what are we talking about?

Common courtesy is politeness that people can usually be expected to show others, whether we know them or not.
— Merriam Webster Dictionary

Definitions

Definition of Manners:
Ways of behaving toward people, esp. ways that are socially correct and show respect for others' comfort and feelings.
— Cambridge Dictionary

Manners are fluid — reflecting the best practices of our time while having timeless and universal principles. Good manners cost nothing to acquire and are a valuable asset.

Emily Post, the "Queen of all things done correctly," said, "Manners are a sensitive awareness of the feelings of others. If you have that awareness, you have good manners, no matter what fork you use."

Definition of Etiquette:

The formal manners or rules that are followed in a social or professional setting. A guideline of how to do things to make others feel comfortable.
— Collins Dictionary

Etiquette is a fancy word for the rules of simple kindness. Etiquette adapts to the diversity of cultural norms and to changing societal norms. But, it is tradition. The key word is **kindness**.

Having money doesn't have anything to do with having good manners. In fact, I've seen some awfully rude wealthy people.

The number one rule is to never be impolite. Being rude is impossible to undo without an apology. And feelings can still remain hurt.

Any other faux pas can be forgiven. Being nice to others is just a kindness that Southerners understand.

So be considerate, and be aware of other's feelings, above your own, and you will come out ahead.

(Here's another part where people are saying, "... And Cindy wrote THAT?")

Whether you bought this book to refresh your memory, pass on the rules to a loved one, or just see how we do things down South, I'm gonna **lay 'em out straight**. I hope to be relatable and hit a humorous but hopeful note. If I am ever snarky or overly sarcastic, I apologize.

My friend Marjorie has a "look" she makes when she sees or hears someone doing something that's incorrect. She simply can't hide it, and it is hilarious. I begged her to let me put her picture in here, but she declined, worried people wouldn't like her. I may post it on social media someday, with her permission, of course.

Not every word is original to me. I've jotted down notes for many years, and read online responses, too. So, if you see something familiar, I'm not claiming it's mine ... it just supports my beliefs.

Etiquette is not about strictness and snobbery. Your hostess won't **clutch her pearls and faint** if you make a mistake. Understanding the lovely rituals and the whys, whens, and hows, will perhaps help you feel more comfortable and confident in any social situation. And that is my wish for you. Your community may not do things exactly the same way as I will present the rules. Use this as a guide. Please don't waste energy battling the rules.

I followed a Facebook page where people posed etiquette questions. Presumably they were seeking guidance on the proper course of action. I often saw, however, respondents advising them to "do what they'd like." I don't think that was the point.

Things are constantly **a changin'**...but a hand written thank you note in polite Southern society is NOT negotiable. **Just sayin'**.

And remember,
as Lewis Grizzard said,
"There's no such thing as being
too Southern."

General Rules

I don't like the word classy because it has a meaning of ~~being uppity~~ superiority. Plus, we don't talk about class. I prefer the word *charming* as it shows grace.

Being seen as a snob is not a virtue I would strive to have. If I don't greet you in Walmart it's because I truly didn't see you.

Simply put, a lady cares about herself and others. Being ladylike does not mean you are snobbish or entitled. Your goal is to put others at ease and to enjoy their company. The best way to achieve this is to have a heart of gratitude. In every thing you do, be thoughtful and deliberate.

To a Southern lady, polite society's standards are important. She makes an effort to attend church, chooses to donate time and money to charity, dresses in a presentable manner, pays her bills on time, and gets married before having children. That's not old fashioned. It's called being a good person. We are taught to just **live right.**

I would rather have a welcoming, gracious home than a perfect home. If you don't have enough glasses at a formal table, substitute and move on. Vintage decor and heirlooms are best used and enjoyed, not just displayed.

One thing I have witnessed in the South is that women compliment one another. I've seen ladies who don't know one another give compliments on another's Derby Day or wedding attire. Just a friendly thumbs-up because we are not intimidated to let a lady know when she's **doin' it right.**

Southern belles carried parasols and wore hoop skirts back in antebellum times. Now it refers to a true Southern lady who has these attributes:
Kindness
Poise
Charisma
Helpfulness
Unpretentiousness
Genteel
Congenial
Gracious

You've heard of Southern Charm? Well, we're proud of it!
Modesty (in dress; as well as in receiving a compliment or
talking about yourself)
Humbleness (I struggle with this one)
Decency
Using decorum
Being delightful
Having a sense of propriety (conforming to proper behavior and
good manners)
Charity (out of respect and courtesy)
Creating harmony instead of discord.

You only have one opportunity to make a first impression, so take a moment to let all of those words sink it. What I'm saying is, how others perceive us in entirely up to us.

Holding onto traditions will help you slow your reactions down, and bring appreciation to your life.

> "The most beautiful voice in the world
> is that of an educated Southern woman."
> – Sir Winston Churchill.

Graciously *accept a compliment* with a "Thank You". It is thoughtless to belittle or deny a compliment. Just say, "Thanks!"

Proper grammar

We actually don't say "**ain't**" much in the South except to make a point during relaxed conversation. Improper grammar is associated with ignorance, and we've worked too hard to break out of that perception. Abuse of the English language is common across the United States. Why would you want to be part of that trend?

And when I thank the employees at a drive-thru, isn't it nicer to hear, "My pleasure!" or "You're welcome," than, "No problem," or "You're good." And what's with this, "Have a good one?"

Southern "rules" for ladies are learned from our mothers, aunts and grandmothers, but this book should make it a little easier.

Once a person thinks it's okay to stray it is easy to **fall off the rails**. For example, your mama will teach you to **put your face on** before **runnin' to town**, so you won't be out in public **lookin' a fright.**

The *worst insult* is to be called **tacky**. Or **coarse**.

And no, I haven't forgotten about manners specific to men. They are just addressed later in the book.

Never put money above manners.

You know the type. They brag and throw their money around to make up for their rudeness.

Fashionably late is not more than 20 minutes. If it's your hairdresser (Sorry, Sandy!), please call. If it's to a gathering, this applies.

Penmanship, fellowship, stewardship are the proverbial characteristics of a lady.

Never chew gum in public.

Fresh breath is important. Have a mint, or better yet, brush your teeth again. When chewing gum, I pretty much look like a cow chewing her cud. So, I keep my gum chewing and singing in the car when I'm by myself. Even to passing cars it is a little frightening.

When you leave a party, always *thank the hosts*. Following up with a note is a kind gesture.

Be the first to *apologize* if you are **at outs** with a friend. No one ever choked to death from swallowing her pride.

It's uncomfortable passing in front of someone *getting to your seat* at the theater or a sporting event. Courteous gentlemen stand to let you pass. Women ~~try to~~ tuck their legs in to give you room. But, do you pass with your bottom passing them or do you face them? I looked it up. In Europe, people pass face to face, but in the U.S.A it is proper for ladies to pass facing away from those seated, while men are to face those they pass.

Ladies don't take off their shoes at a party. Ever. Do not dance barefooted. Wear your shoes to break them in before a big event. Select a pair you can wear for several hours. Or take a pair of flats in your handbag. I may be crippled the next day, but you will ~~NEVER EVER~~ not see me without shoes in public.

Being satisfied with your life will bring you happiness.

If you want something, work for it. We always want something we cannot have... like Chick-fil-A on a Sunday. (And if you don't know to ask for the sauce they only keep in the back, your happiness has been deprived.)

Never smoke on the street or cross a room with a lit cigarette.

Refrain from putting a cigarette in in your mouth before your lighter is ready, too. Talking with an unlit cigarette bouncing between your lips is without a doubt unattractive. Standing on the street with a cigarette...this is every form of tackiness.

Be kind. As your grandmother said, *"You'll catch more flies with honey than with vinegar."*

She also said, *"Pretty is as pretty does."*

Now, before you begin feeling overwhelmed, here are a couple of thoughts:

1. The rules aren't as important as your kindness, your generosity of time and your smile. And those things are free.
2. You don't need the perfect house to entertain. It's your home, your style, and your happy place. So, invite those you love to share time with you even if you don't know what to do about a centerpiece and you can't plan a perfect menu. It's most important to be welcoming and to be together.

I love owning my grandmothers' china and silver. I don't use it daily, but for holidays and entertaining I am pleased to share its history... the delicate porcelain china from a Limoges factory that no longer exists, pink and green Depression glass, the weight of the silverware, and the joy of watching my grand twins help set the table.

If people feel special while in your home, your hospitality provides the opportunity to create memories and traditions.

And to visitors to the South, be warned that we love to display family photos. Our homes are the scrapbooks of our lives.

Southern Hospitality

For five years our church had the **most precious** group come down from Colorado Springs. That week of mission work meant the world to our small Presbyterian congregation. Our aim was to praise The Lord, help others, and show our guests some **good ol' Southern Hospitality**. This meant feeding them our best Southern meals, sharing our bug spray, inviting them into our homes, and showing off "all things Southern." We'd take them out to shoot guns, enjoy fireworks, ride four-wheelers, and help them with their mission projects, painting, building, and bible school.

The first year that they came down, they had watched *The Help* to prepare. I was flabbergasted. We are no longer the Old South. *Duck Dynasty* would have actually been more appropriate!

Southerners love to talk to total strangers.

And we're polite to people who wait on us. I cannot imagine not thanking someone. While on a bicycle tour in Maine a few years ago, I asked the lady behind the counter at an antique mall "how she was doin'?" She literally just looked at me. She didn't understand why I was asking her. Weird.

We love our families, our faith, our football and our food.

Southern ladies *never return a dish empty*. This is a difficult one for me because I simply don't like to cook. But the rule is to return a casserole dish or Tupperware with some sort of treat inside. It's polite and it's tradition.

Hostess gifts are nice. If you are staying with a friend, take a small gift to show your appreciation for their hospitality — a local gourmet food, a simple floral bouquet, anything to show you are a thoughtful and appreciative guest.

During a *toast*, if you are being toasted, don't drink. Instead return the toast with a thank you toast to those who toasted you.

Cheers, Prost, santé, chin chin, Sláinte —

The *cheek kiss* in America is right to right. Once. In Europe, it's twice.

Why the *pineapple*? Ship captains would sail into Charleston and place a pineapple on their wrought iron gates to signify they were home and welcoming visitors to see the wares from their travels. The pineapple became a welcome symbol of hospitality.

I first experienced the pineapple symbol in Colonial Williamsburg, Virginia, and love it to this day; especially because I was blessed for many years to represent tourism and hospitality for the state of Arkansas.

At the Table

Make your *conversation* light and bright and don't overpower the table. Share the conversation. Ask questions and be attentive to others to make shared time pleasant. (Daddy Don just chortled.)

While seated for a meal, if you must *sneeze*, please turn your head and sneeze into your elbow as opposed to your hand. If it comes too quickly, use your napkin, and by all means, turn your head. Then excuse yourself. I think we all finally learned this during the Coronapocolypse of 2020.

It necessary, only *cough* into your left hand (but, best, your elbow), as your right hand is used for shaking hands.

Compliment the hostess. Whether it's the food, the table decor, her home, or her attire, compliment her. *Thank* your hosts. Twice. Once as you depart and again with a handwritten note.

As a guest in someone's home, it is kind to *mention a food allergy ahead of time*, especially if it is an intimate setting. But if you don't like grits, are vegan, or are watching your carbs, simply pick your way around the menu without bringing it into the spotlight. Your hostess doesn't have time to change the menu last minute.

Don't "graze" when food is served buffet-style. **Fix a plate** and then eat. Please refrain from eating "hunched over" the dips like you're eating from a trough.

All the best hostesses know there's plenty of food back in the kitchen.

How to set a proper table:

The sharp side of *the knife* faces the plate. It goes on the right with the spoon to the right of the knife.

Forks are on the left, with the *napkin.*

Dessert forks or dessert spoons can be found above the plate.

A simple rule for your *silverware* is to use the "outside-in" method, working your way closer to the plate with each course.

The *glasses* are on your right, above the knife and spoon. Make an "okay" sign, and the "d" stands for drinks. The *bread plate (and salad plate)* are on your left. Make an "okay" sign with your left hand, and the "b" stands for bread (plate).

It is okay to cut your salad if needed. My mother often served a wedge salad, and it had to be cut. They are quite popular today, ~~and ridiculously expensive~~ but when I was growing up, it was just easy for her.

The continental method (European) of holding silverware has the fork always in the left hand, tines facing down, to stab the food. We switch hands after using a knife and eat with the fork tines facing up in our right hand.

Please note than when setting a table, there's no place for the *cellphone.*

What about *blowing on food?*

The hostess has spent a lot of energy making sure your meal is served delicious to her standard. If the food is too hot to eat, take the hint and patiently wait until it cools. But don't get me wrong. We've all taken a bite of fried green tomato or pizza and burned our mouths.

Also, it is considered rude to add *salt and pepper* before tasting the food. One must assume the cook seasoned it correctly.

It is incorrect to *cut* all of your meat before eating, unless you are still a child. And, as you cut off pieces of meat, make them small so you can continue the conversation without a lot of chewing and swallowing… or choking. Nobody wants to **hightail it** to the emergency room during a dinner party

How to remove unwanted food from your mouth:

First of all, be discrete. Remove the food in the same manner it went into your mouth. If you put it in with a fork, spit it into your fork. A pit or bone is therefore removed with your fingers. (Note, I've tried this and it is very awkward trying to remove food with a fork. For one thing, it shows. Do whatever you can to be discreet. I'm just providing the rule.)

Serve from the left. Retrieve from the right.

Do not scrape and pile *your plates* in an attempt to help the server. I wish restaurants would train their staff to refrain from removing anything except the salad plate during the meal. When they clear the condiments, the other's plates, and keep asking if I'm finished, it really ~~gets irritating~~ becomes a nuisance.

Many people think couples should be seated together at a dinner party. Actually, they should be seated apart with men and women alternating to create lively conversation. The guest of honor is always seated to the right of the host. I've learned quite a bit while writing this book…I would've tended to put the guest of honor at the head of the table.

Sitting "Delta Style" (Because I live in the Mississippi River Delta of Arkansas) on a night out with friends, means the men and women sit on opposite ends of the table. We do this among friends. After years of marriage, we're all happy to see one another, but there's not much pretense at the table about sitting as couples. The men typically talk about hunting and farming while we're talking about children and social events.

Yes, we talk about world events as well.

And on the ride home, our husbands want to know what we women discussed, but not the specifics. Just like we don't really want to hear about fertilizer and antler width.

Your aim as a hostess is to bless your guests, not impress. Lively conversation, scented candles around the house (but not on the table), flowers, a special menu, lamps illuminating the room, nice background music — will make them thankful for the opportunity to spend time in your home.

Ladies, it is a courtesy to *discreetly remove your lipstick* before eating at a fine restaurant. Lipstick trace on the napkins and glassware is **the devil** for restaurant personnel.

Occasionally, a need will arise when you will *send your food back*. It is not necessary to be ~~tacky~~ apologetic, but be appreciative when it is corrected. When initiating this activity, be specific and kind. And remember, it's not the server's fault if your meal is overcooked, too salty, too fatty, etc.

We love *mason jars* because our grandmothers used them to put up jelly and pickles and such. They're perfect for canning some homemade salsa, holding a few flowers, or just used as a drinking glass.

Eat *soup* by pushing the spoon away from yourself. "As little ships sail out to sea, I push my spoon away from me." Don't slurp. And again, if it is too hot, just wait a bit.

Don't leave your *spoon* in the soup or cereal bowl. Teach your children by saying, "Man overboard!" to prompt them to place the spoon on their saucer.

Learn to use a *pasta spoon* with your fork when eating spaghetti. This method of twirling the pasta is used in part, but not all, of Italy. Unless you're four years old, slurping spaghetti is considered poor manners. (But when my five-year-old grandtwins, Olivia and James, reenact that scene from *Lady and the Tramp*, it really is hilarious!)

Have you ever wondered what to do with *citrus fruit* after you squeeze it into your drink? First of all, never leave it hanging on your glass. That just looks ridiculous. Whether you place a squeezed or unsqueezed lemon on the edge of your plate (not on the table) or drop it in the glass, it is your choice.

Please, if you're not using it, don't leave it on the rim of your margarita.

The napkin.

Always in your lap. It is correct to place your napkin in your lap immediately after being seated. Place it on your chair if you excuse yourself during a meal. (But the British say it goes on the back of your chair). At a fine restaurant, if you place it on the table, the server will refold it and place it on your chair for you to find when you return. At the conclusion of the meal, pinch your napkin in the middle and place it to the left of your plate.

In a fancy restaurant, the server will bring you a black napkin if you are wearing black to keep fibers off of your slacks or skirt.

Fold a square napkin in half, with the fold at your knees. Fold the top back from your knees, forming a pocket to catch crumbs if they fall in your lap.

The chair

When you have finished your meal, please push your chair in when you rise to exit.

The silverware.

When you have finished eating, place them next to each other on the plate. That signals the wait staff that you have completed your meal. While eating, keep your silverware on the plate, never placed again on the table.

Candles

Lit candles should not be considered as centerpieces in the daytime. Save them for evening entertaining. And before putting candles in the candlesticks, light the wicks briefly, then blow out the flame. I don't know why there is a rule about unburnt taper wicks, but there is.

Wine Etiquette

White wines are held by the stem in order to keep them cool. Red wines served in a rounder glass may be held by the bowl.

And some other things:

Do not ever say, "Garçon!" or "Waiter!" to get the staff's attention. (They used to show this in cartoons). It is considered to be rude. Just lift a finger and try to make eye contact.

Refrain from using bread to **sop up** the delicious sauce on your plate — especially in a formal situation. Now, I know sometimes that you absolutely can't think of anything better than **soppin' that sauce**. I'm providing the rule. That's why I said "refrain."

~~Never~~ Please, do not use a *toothpick* at the table. Grab one on your way out of a restaurant and use it in the vehicle. Or go to the restroom. At home, or as a guest in someone's home, go to the powder room to remove anything from your teeth.

Never consider *blowing your nose* at the table. Just don't do it. Ever. If your nose is "drippy," you may discreetly blot.

It is all right to quickly reapply *lipstick*, but don't freshen the rest of your makeup at the table. Excuse yourself and visit the powder room.

When eating, keep one *hand in your lap*.

In the South, we eat corn on the cob, fried chicken, and pizza with our hands.

The "no elbows on the table" rule applies only when you are actually eating. Putting your elbows on the table is acceptable, at home or with friends, if you are not using utensils. If you are at a business luncheon or dining with royalty... no elbows. However, it's a good idea to teach your children the song, "Mike, Mike, if you're able. Get your elbows off the table. This is not a horse's stable, this is just a dining table."

When in a restaurant, *closing your menu* signals the server that you are ready to order. Thank goodness, the man ordering for a lady is obsolete. But it is correct for the woman to be encouraged to order first.

What is a *charger*? It's just a large plate, serving a similar purpose to a placemat that the dinner plate sits upon. It is decoration.

Men's hats at the table are addressed later.

Southern Supper Club

When we were "young married" we had Supper Club — mostly because we had a shared lack of money. There weren't that many restaurants in our small town, and setting a date ensured that we would get together socially once a month. We had potluck meals; we had theme suppers; we had a box social; and we had ~~pretty raucous~~ scavenger hunts. Those were some of our pre-kid memories. I think a little in-town **drinkin' & drivin'** was prevalent back in those days.

Apparently, several Southern cities have supper clubs where restaurants and chefs set up dates for customers to come dine. That's much more exclusive than what we did. And it sounds marvelous. Ours was our first attempt at entertaining.

Entertaining, Southern Style

Our homes are where we best enjoy time with friends. A *well-stocked bar* is essential, and appreciated.

We often serve *buffet-style* when entertaining at home. A few recommendations are:

Place the plates at the beginning of the spread, napkins and silverware at the end of the line.

Try to vary the height, and intersperse flowers among the dishes, making access easy to your guests.

Label the offerings to make identification easy.

Put iced tea and water to the side, and offer to deliver it to the table for your guests.

On my first visit to Natchez, I asked the docent the difference between a veranda and a porch. She replied, "If you're sipping a mint julep you're on the veranda. If you're drinking sweet tea or lemonade you're on the porch. If you're not drinking anything, it's a shame!" Love that.

"No Southern home is complete without a picture of a magnolia," was shared with me on my first visit to a Louisiana plantation home. When I see a magnolia painting, I can just hear that person's Southern drawl.

Ladies gathering together used to be called a **hen party.** I love that "girls' night out" is now officially acceptable.

"Friendsgiving!" What a splendid idea to have Thanksgiving with friends before heading home to spend it with family.

And Galantine's Day (February 13th or 15th) is "ladies celebrating ladies," according to Leslie Knope on *Parks & Recreation.* There are even Galantine's cards and paper products available now.

Speaking of family, I have the best. Really. I think we are the envy of our peers. My in-laws are the best. We absolutely look forward to holidays together. ~~It might be because drinking is involved~~, but they really are so pleasant. We celebrate Thanksgiving twice in the same day. We eat around noon, giving thanks for our family, health, and blessings. Then the men go out to the woods and the ladies **pile up** to watch a movie. That evening we eat turkey sandwiches and ~~fight over~~ devour the last of Granny's dressing.

Each Christmas Eve we gather at my brother-in-law's after the church service and we enjoy hors d'oeuvres, chili, some holiday ham, and Delta hot tamales. This is casual and relaxing.

On Christmas Day, everyone comes to our home where we have an amazing salad, twice-baked potatoes, and grilled steaks. It's the best menu and low stress. I know friends who recreate the menu from Thanksgiving for Christmas. With all the last-minute gift-wrapping and guests, the steak menu has worked well for us.

We Smith daughters-in-law like to tease our mother-in-law that she sure is lucky her sons **"married up."** In truth, we are all fortunate.

Naturally, place settings and formal dining make holidays more fun. I enjoy inviting girlfriends over mid-week, just to enjoy a simple lunch menu. It gives me the opportunity to use my good china, table linens, crystal, and flowers from my garden.

At Christmastime, I change out all of my glasses and dishes to enjoy my Spode Christmas china. I have Easter plates and pumpkin plates as well.

If a guest brings wine, serve it.

If you take wine and your hostess doesn't serve it, consider it a gift and never ask for it back.

And in all your entertaining, ladies, *avoid posting photos where you are consuming alcohol.* Just put the glass down. It cheapens the photo.

It's always best to drink beer from a cup or glass, instead of the can or bottle, at a more formal gathering.

In college "function" photos, we were always taught to put our drink down on the nearest table, and to never, ever dance with a drink in hand. I'm talking about at a wedding reception. Not in a bar. Yes, I know there's concern now about being drugged. Just get another drink, I say!

Housewarmings and Open Houses

If you have just purchased or built a new home, and would like to share your excitement with your friends, have an *open house*. Invite them to come over for a quick bite, or an evening, and they can see what you have done.

If friends offer to give you a *housewarming*, they are to mail invitations and provide the food. Essentially, they are giving you a shower.

You ~~cannot~~ should not give yourself a housewarming, because it is gauche to ever expect gifts.

An *"At Home"* is an invitation to stop by and visit, for a short time, during specific time period. This could be during the peak beauty of your gardens, New Year's Day, Christmas afternoon, etc. Usually just a libation of sorts is served. I've received invitations that simply say, "At Home with Richard and Betsy, New Year's Day, 11-1."

Preparing the Perfect Guest Room

Having a welcoming guest room is such a gift for all who stay in your home. Try to provide the softest sheets and best bed linens you can afford. If I were to ever win the lottery, I would have fresh ironed sheets on my beds daily. I'm passionate about down pillows, although some folks have allergies.

Amenities to make their stay pleasant include:

Having an extension cord so your guests don't have to search for a receptacle to charge their phones

Providing water at the bedside

Providing your Wi-Fi password

Letting them know where the thermostat is located and offering an extra blanket

Having a small vase with fresh flowers in the room

Lip gloss, lotion, Kleenex, blow dryer, shampoo and conditioner, and even a facemask can be nice, even if not needed by your guests

The Golden Rule and Not Burning Bridges

It's so easy to be kind. Smile and you'll get a smile in return. "Do unto others as you shall have them do unto you." Give a helping hand to others. Well-bred Southerners know the phrase, "Every door, every time." We hold the door for the elderly, disabled, and anyone within a few feet of the door.

There's a lot of talk out there about Karma and wishing you hadn't wasted your positive energy on others. Really? You wake up every day and can make it good or bad. Do you honestly regret having been nice and investing time in another person? I should think not. Not everyone reacts the same way that you do or may be the kind of friend you need. So, my Mom taught me not to burn my bridges.

"Make new friends, but keep the old. One is silver and the other's gold." This wise Scouting song still rings true.

So often in life friendships fizzle. But that doesn't mean they have ended. Your life and activities have gone in a different direction. That sure doesn't mean a friendship needs to be terminated. There's no need for unkind words and permanence.

I like these:

Holding a grudge doesn't make you strong, it makes you bitter.

Forgiving doesn't make you weak, it sets you free.

Davie Willis

It's hard to forgive, but it's harder not to.

Be respectful, even to hateful, nasty people, because your momma raised you better.

And as mama always said, "Kill them with kindness, and bury them with a smile."

Simple Tips For Dressing

Natalie came downstairs in a short skirt while in high school, prior to her National Honor Society induction, inquiring if her outfit was appropriate. It was not. That gave us the opportunity to go through her closet and discuss what to wear and when. She commented later about her friend, whose skirt that day was both too tight and too short. She was grateful we had had "the talk." Always wear a longer skirt when sitting on a stage. And cross your legs at the ankles, not at your knees. You'll never see anyone from the royal family with her legs crossed.

A Southern lady knows these tips:

The higher the hem, the lower the heel, ~~unless you WANT to look like a hooker~~

Dress *tastefully,* appropriate for the occasion

Cleavage after five o'clock only, and please, consider the circumstances. What's up with these news anchors dressed like they're going out? And with **the sisters** all pushed up?

Leg OR *décolletage.* Together is vulgar. A short slip dress that is cut down to your navel leaves little to the imagination.

Let's discuss this further.... use subtlety to create a sexy look. You may want to draw a little attention with a bare leg, or a tad more cleavage, but a little mystery is far sexier than just showing it all. At the office, shirt cleavage should not be deeper than 4 inches from your collarbone. Never let your ~~belly button~~ midriff show. Wear a camisole. Office blouses without sleeves should cover your shoulders. Refrain from wearing spaghetti straps. Best to wear a suit jacket for formal meetings.

If your most private body parts or their outline shows under the fabric, you **might oughta** rethink your outfit. Same thing if you have trouble sitting, bending over, putting the outfit on, or getting it off. And if people are looking at your body before looking at your face, you should go find another outfit. A Southern lady desires beauty over looking sexy.

There's a right and a wrong way to *enter a vehicle*. Some things just can't be unseen. We 80's girls remember *Glamour "Don'ts."*

Pearls are a welcomed gift, whether given by your fiancé, grandmother or parents. Pearls go with everything in the South, even blue jeans.

Save your best jewelry for evening.

This includes diamond studs, but I love them.

Avoid wearing three or four pieces of *matching jewelry*. Ring and necklace, or earrings and bracelet look best. The Queen of England wears a full parure. That's the necklace, earrings and more that match her crown. For us, less is best.

With a beaded dress, pare down the jewelry. As Coco Chanel guided us — before you leave the house, take something off — a necklace, or whatever. Don't overdo the accessories.

Find a *signature scent* and enjoy. French perfumeries are designed to help find a woman's scent, as the essences react differently with each person. Do not overindulge.

I lived in Boulder my freshman year of college. I couldn't get over how the girls simply never dressed up. The wind was dreadful, but the natural look was a little too sparse for me. Guys there loved my accent. It was easy to have conversations and make friends. But after a year I transferred to Arkansas, and eventually married my good Southern guy.

So, **big hair** is a Southern thing. Nowhere on earth do girls compare to college girls in the SEC. We're just taught to look our best. We like creams and perfume and we get our hair styled regularly. We dress for church and to go out to dinner, and to football games and to the horse races. After all, when are we supposed to get to wear all of our stylish clothes?

We spend a lot of money on hairspray and lotions. But it's worth it to a Southern girl to try to look our best. And y'all know, that 100% humidity keeps us on our toes.

That's not to say I don't occasionally look like Ouiser from *Steel Magnolias*. If I'm working in my yard and decide I need something from Walmart, I just fly out there **lookin' a mess** to get my supplies. It never fails that I'll run into someone who undoubtedly thinks I've been ill. Hopefully, the next time I see them, remembering how ~~dreadful~~ I looked the last time they saw me, they'll say, "Oh my gosh, you look incredible!"

And let's not even mention how my gray was **shinin'** during that unfortunate pandemic time.

Fingernails

Clean. If polished, never chipped. Shorter wins over longer and natural wins over fake.

A Southern lady knows how to get her hands dirty, but keeps her nails clean.

Toenails should always be polished if your toes are showing. That means you can take a short break in the winter.

Oh, the *bra straps*. ~~I know you know better.~~

Please wear a camisole if your blouse is light and transparent; or if it gaps at the buttons. The cute multi-strap bras under sportswear are a fashion statement. You know what I'm referring to about tacky bra straps.

White shoes? Never after Labor Day or before Easter. This is a Southern thing, as it is the best way for us to remember what season it is.

As for wearing white, the color signifies summer, unless it is "winter white." That's the rule. It includes white slacks, dresses and purses, too. But girls are wearing their white jeans a little longer if it's still 85 degrees. I'm not saying it's right, but I'm seeing it. Our weather can drop as much as 40 degrees in a day, so plan your wardrobe accordingly.

Suede shoes obviously shouldn't be worn during poor weather. They used to be appropriate only after Labor Day, but now light colors can be worn year-round.

Any shoes that show your toes should not be worn with pantyhose.

Athleisure wear are these trendy yoga/exercise clothes that **fit young things** just wear all day. I envy them.

But leggings?

There is a saying: "Small children, drunk people, and leggings never lie." Ladies, please only wear leggings under a looooong top, being sure to cover your bottom. As for yoga pants... a store in my small town had a sign once that said, "plus-sized yoga pants." Uh, no. Unless you just don't care.

Oh, and just never wear *white to a wedding* (or to the rehearsal dinner). It's the bride's color. I once looked up at a wedding reception and saw a beautiful girl in white out on the dance floor. I was appalled until I realized the bride had changed from her wedding gown to a **darlin'** white dress in preparation for leaving her reception!

In Victorian times, and of course at funerals, black symbolized mourning. For many years it was taboo to wear black to weddings. (It still is, in England). Back then, most weddings were in the morning or early afternoon, so naturally the color was considered incorrect apparel. In modern times black is perfectly acceptable for a wedding as the reception typically overlaps the cocktail hour. Also, have you tried buying a dress appropriate for evening lately? Half of them are black. So, buy the LBD and don't worry.

I was taught not to wear a *watch* to a formal affair. It signals that you are concerned with the time, which can be construed as an insult to the host. For gentlemen in tuxes, place a dressier watch on your left arm, if necessary, as you shake with the right hand. And ladies, unless you have a delicate dress watch, just wear your better jewelry and leave the iWatch at home, even if you'll have to guess your steps "earned" from all that dancin'.

Ladies carry *handbags*. A purse is for loose change. I always have trouble remembering what it should be called. I like when our grandmothers referred to it as a pocketbook.

It's kinda like the sofa/couch debate.

A *clutch* should be carried in front of you with both hands and fingers facing downward, or with one hand hanging down. According to Royal rules you should never carry a clutch ~~in your armpit~~ tucked under your arm. I'll remember that next time I have tea with Kate and William.

I'm all about a crossbody bag, especially when out shopping. It keeps my hands free for selection. And I don't carry much anyhow — billfold, lipstick, nail file, mints, phone, pen, and Kleenex.

The rule is to never place your handbag on the floor, especially in a public restroom. ("Purse on the floor, money out the door.")

In a restaurant, if I hang it from my chair, though, the waitress can easily knock it off. Not sure what the procedure is here. It's always handy if there's an extra chair to place it on. If small, I place it behind my back.

I used to make Taylor put his cap under his chair, and we left quite a few behind. I appreciate bars that have hooks located underneath the counter.

When you are a guest in someone's home, it is polite to place your handbag and coat on the foot of the master bedroom bed if the hostess does not offer to place it elsewhere. Do not **sling it** just anywhere that's handy. She doesn't want handbags on every surface. Hosts typically offer to hang your wrap in the coat closet, but foyers are built differently now. Also, my front hall closet is full of table linens. Hmmmmmm.

As a guest, feel free to use those fancy hand towels (**show towels**), that at your own home everyone knows not to touch.

So, what do all of those *invitations* mean for ladies? The best way to know what to wear is to look at the invitation. If it is engraved, dress **to the nines**. If it is picnic plaid, it's sure to be casual. The location of the event can also be an indication of what to wear if it's not specified on the invitation itself. *Black Tie Optional, Cocktail Attire, Garden Party, and Business Casual* all require different attire.

Oscar Wilde said, "You can never be overdressed or overeducated." I once saw a man at a church wedding in cargo pants, hiking boots, and a polo shirt. I'm sure that's the best he had, but I blame his mama and his wife for not getting him **fixed up proper.**

Don knows I expect him to wear his black suit to all weddings and funerals, no questions asked.

And if you're ever not sure, just call the host/hostess of the event and inquire about what they will be wearing. Don doesn't mind wearing khakis and a sports jacket, but not when other guys are in jeans.

It takes me about 45 minutes to get dressed — if I have already decided what to wear… and if I don't get distracted by wandering into the laundry room (where I begin to fold and sort and next thing I know I'm late.) **Truth be told**, when a woman tells a man she'll be ready in five minutes, she's referring to the same five-minute span that is left in a televised football game.

Delta Casual is dressy enough to feel good about your appearance, but still comfortable. According to Mississippi's Delta Magazine, Delta Casual is defined as *attire or style in social circles that's not dressy but inherently tasteful.*

Personal Appearance

A guy has never liked a girl for her makeup.

I think ladies are much more obsessed about make-up trends than men ever consider.

It is a good idea to wear less makeup as you age. We've all talked, distractedly, with the older lady at Church. You know, the one with pronounced base makeup and crooked eyebrows?

Young ladies follow all of the eyeliner trends. But liner all around the eyes makes more mature ladies look older. Believe me.

A word about self-tanners. Orange. This is the color to avoid. Avoid being referred to as "Dorito girl" or an Oompa Loompa, by simply using a better product, and using it sparingly. If you like spray tans, dial down the darkness factor, similarly to getting the smaller size when getting a ~~boob job~~ breast augmentation. I advise you to use sunscreen, especially on your face. And use the leftover on the back of your hands. You'll be glad to delay those age spots which appear later in life.

I always wanted to be one of those chic older women who wore her hair carefully smoothed into a ponytail. Unfortunately, Natalie informed me that you simply must be thin to be chic and pull this off. I tend to agree, as I typically look like I should be doing yard work or housework when my hair is in a ponytail.

My husband says, "I've never seen a girl whose beauty was enhanced by a tattoo."

Do you stoop or bend? It is proper, and better for your back, to stoop when picking something up. Unfortunately, I tend to bend. It's not a pretty sight. Learn from me.

I kinda wish God had sent me a message when I was about to "peak." Here I am, rocking along at age 22, not realizing I looked the absolutely best ever, and I didn't even know it. I may have worn a bikini more, or taken more time just to enjoy being young. But that's just not how life works. But let me add, I don't regret getting older. I just regret not looking as good!

Part Two
The Wedding Section

Traditions

The Bridal Portrait

A Southern belle should always have her bridal portrait made. It can hang in your mother's home until you choose to have in it a place of honor in your own home. (In the South, we get our picture "made", not "taken"). It's a lovely tradition to display the portrait at the couple's reception.

The Bow Bouquet

At showers, save all uncut bows from the gifts and make a bouquet. Each cut ribbon signifies a child to be born, so Southern brides make every effort to pull the ribbons off of shower gifts. A friend at rehearsal carries this bouquet as she stands in for the bride. The bride sits in a pew and observes the rehearsal of the ceremony, without participating, as that is considered bad luck. She doesn't walk down the aisle until the following day, when she walks to her groom.

The House Party or Honorary Bridesmaids

These are close friends of the bride, but not quite close enough to make the bridesmaids' cut. They dress similarly and sit in a designated pew. They are asked to help with the bride's guest book, and in years past, to cut the cake, serve punch, pass out the programs and perhaps the rice bags.

Since Southerners do things "big," sharing your day with all friends being honored is a big thing. (In 1981 I had one bridesmaid, my childhood best friend, and she made her own dress. Yes, things were simpler then.)

My husband calls the House Party the "B Team." Our good friend (age 68) happened to wear a coordinating dress to another friend's daughter's wedding, and he kept asking her if she was part of the house party!

How the bride asks her friends to be bridesmaids has become a thing. Bottles of champagne, personalized cookies and more arrive at the door, asking, "Will you be my bridesmaid?"

The Charm Cake

The charm cake at the bridal tea or bridesmaids' luncheon is a lovely tradition. Silver charms on satin ribbon are placed inside the layer cake when it is frosted. The bridesmaids pull them out to place on a necklace or charm bracelet — and each charm has significance.

Mississippi Magazine has a spring edition filled with wedding descriptions. I've looked forward to it for years. When Natalie married I wanted some *memorable traditions*.
These included:

Her great grandmother, Grandmére, made a satin wedding gown after she and my mother spotted the design in the window of a fashion house in Paris' haute couture district in 1953. My mother wore it in 1955 when my parents married. I wore it in 1981 with very little adjustment. We had it shortened for Natalie to wear at their rehearsal dinner in 2010.

Wedding guests threw wheat as she and Josh departed the church. Don had grown the wheat on our family farm; a French tradition.

Pinned to her bridal bouquet, she carried Grandmère's cameo.

She and Josh were married in the same sanctuary as Don and I were, 29 years later.

She wore my pearl bracelet, and a lucky sixpence in her shoe. I've seen a locket with a beloved grandparent's picture pinned inside the groom's jacket, or carried on the bride's bouquet. I've also seen an embroidered heart sewn onto the back of the groom's tie.

New tradition: Place a bottle of wine and love letters to one another in a wooden box and nail it shut. When the couple has their *first fight*, they open the box to remember their love for one another.

Burying the bourbon

One month prior to the wedding, bury a bottle of unopened bourbon facedown in the exact spot you plan to recite your vows. This will ensure perfect weather on your wedding day, when you will dig it up and enjoy.

Marrying on the half hour

This is considered good luck.

Rain on your wedding day

I think they tell brides that this is good luck so they won't have a **come-apart.**

Gifting the Couple

Shower gifts are the essentials. Every newlywed needs a seasoned cast-iron skillet, a mixer, an iced tea pitcher... and a deviled egg serving plate.

Wedding gifts are the finer gifts. This can be candlesticks, crystal stemware, a fine china pattern, silver trays and flatware, or antiques. A Southern bride will be pleased she selected julep cups as part of her registry. They are the perfect beverage cup for entertaining and can double as a floral container.

Back in the day the bride's mother's friends, or the church ladies would give a small **kitchen shower.** It was appropriate to gift some baking dishes, a cookbook, a hand mixer, etc. Skip to this century and showers have become more elaborate. It is perfectly acceptable to send your wedding gift to a shower ~~and call it good~~ as two expensive gifts are not necessary. Giving one gift or two is left to the discretion of the giver. Gifts can be delivered to the home anytime.

Please try not to take gifts with you to the actual ceremony or to the reception. This just creates another job for the family to get it to the couple later.

The trousseau

These are the clothes the bride wears to her parties and into her first years of marriage. They are as important as rush clothes used to be. (Now they make everyone dress alike, ~~which is crazy~~.)

The bride-to-be always wants to look her best at the parties given to the couple. Currently brides are wearing all white to their parties. I've seen some lovely dresses, but it concerns me that they will have very few chances to wear them again, as only the bride wears white.

The trousseau also refers to her household linens and other necessities.

Hope chests have become a thing of the past, but they were filled with hand-embroidered towels and other niceties needed to begin a home.

The engagement announcement

Traditionally, only the bride's picture was in the newspaper for an engagement announcement. A more modern announcement includes the groom with the bride. This has become acceptable because friends like to see who is betrothed. The Southern code for engagement announcement photos is still a studio headshot of the bride only. If a couple chooses to use a photo of them together, it should be discouraged for it to be one of them cuddling. And posing to show the engagement ring ~~is just tacky~~ may want to be avoided.

The displaying of the wedding gifts in the family home is a Southern tradition. However, they should not be displayed with the gift cards, which enable **little ol' ladies** to see how much their neighbors spent.

The mother of the bride invites cherished (older) friends to come see the gifts. This practice is called a *Sip 'n See*. (See newer version in baby section.) Unfortunately, this tradition is becoming outdated for several reasons. The first is that many couples won't be living in the bride's hometown and it is just easier to take the gifts on to their new home. The second is room constraints. Natalie's were displayed in our game room upstairs, which made it difficult when having overnight guests on the wedding weekend.

Many couples begin using gifts prior to the wedding. This could get complicated if one partner calls the whole thing off. It's difficult to return opened and used gifts, but no excuse.

Prompt thank you notes.

Handwritten. Personal. Please make sure to include the return address.

Hostess Gifts

This new trend of the couple gifting their hosts, is very thoughtful, but does not replace writing a kind note. It is also nice for the mothers to write thank you notes to their friends who host wedding parties for their children.

The Receiving Line

The receiving line is not antiquated. It is the perfect way to greet the couple and parents (hosts). It doesn't have to last for hours, but it certainly puts the guests at ease. I much prefer attending a reception where I have met the hosts. It's disquieting to have to hunt them down to meet them and let them know you appreciate being included.

The Monogram

When I married, the woman simply used her husband's monogram on household items.

The Colonial Williamsburg style is husband/LAST/wife.

The modern style is wife/LAST/husband.

The important thing to remember is to refrain from using the monogram on cookies, napkins, etc. until the reception. Your new monogram should not be used at showers, as you are not yet married.

Taking his last name, keeping yours, or combining with a hyphen — your business. Do what pleases you. No big deal.

The saying is, "no matter how many marriages, a Southern lady always wears white." But I did encourage those who asked me, to tone it down after the first wedding. For instance, a bride never registers twice. But if a man remarries and his bride has never been married, she is subject to all the same courtesy as a first-time couple.

Who Pays for What?

The **Groom** (and/or his family) pays for:
> The bride's engagement and wedding rings
> The marriage license
> The officiant's fee and travel expenses
> Bride's bouquet and going-away corsage
> Flowers for the mothers and grandmothers
> Boutonnieres, (gloves, optional), and ties for the men of the wedding party
> Wedding gift for the bride

Limousine expense leaving reception, or for the day
Wedding night accommodations
The Honeymoon
Groom's cake (Southern tradition)
Gifts for the best man and groomsmen
Lodging for groomsmen from out of town
Rehearsal dinner

The **Bride**'s family pays for:
Church and reception venue rental
Cake, catering, and beverages for the reception
Invitations, announcements, save-the-dates, and
stationery (And in 2020, we had to add change-the-dates)
Services of a wedding consultant
Photography for the engagement, bridal portrait,
ceremony, and reception (and then freely offers the
photos to the groom's family)
Floral arrangements for the church and reception
Bouquets for bridesmaids
Corsages for special helpers, house party, etc.
Wedding ceremony music
Reception music/band
Limousine for bride and family to the church, and cars for
transportation of bridal party
Gifts for the bridal party
Lodging for bridal party
Security and insurance
Wedding favors

The **Bride** pays for:
The groom's wedding ring.
Wedding gift for the groom.

Now folks, this is negotiable. If anyone is more
comfortable paying for something and asks to do so, that's fine.
But it's handy to have something to go by, so I hope this helps.
I have been to many receptions where the groom's family **foots
the bill** for the alcohol because the bride's parents don't drink.

If you are trying to stay within a budget, sit your daughter down and ask her to list what three aspects are the most important to her. It may be the dress, the wedding flowers, and the band. For you, it may be the music, the reception fare, and the invitations. Then you can each give input in planning.

How to cut costs:
A smaller guest list
Unlined envelopes
An afternoon reception
A morning wedding
No videographer
Family member as photographer
Wine and beer at the reception instead of open bar
DJ instead of a live band (But please don't hire one of those irritating, "talky" DJs. Folks just wanna celebrate.)

My mother said my wedding expenses were $2600. This even included family flying in. Natalie's port-a-palace cost that same amount. Go figure.

The First Look

Let's talk about *the first look*. You know what I think? I think the groom should not see his bride until she comes down the aisle. I love to look at the groom when the doors open. I like to see his true emotions.

The trend now is to have the couple privately see one another prior to the ceremony. By sharing this moment prior to the ceremony, they can take all of the photos with their attendants and be free after the ceremony to head to the reception. I'm not steadfast in my feelings against this. I tend to like tradition, because I'm OLD. I've seen some pretty moving wedding videos of the first look, too.

But to me, it's about the ceremony more than everything else. It's perfectly acceptable to take photos after the ceremony while your guests travel to the reception. Cherish this time with family. I, for one, know that the wedding party dreads showing up at ten for a five o'clock wedding, to allow plenty of time for the pre-ceremony photo shoot. And if children are part of the ceremony, that's more opportunity for meltdowns by the flower girl and ring bearer.

The Bride's Role

Be humble, kind, and appreciative... and get those thank you notes written.

The Role of Bridesmaids (Attendants)

I have never been more moved than when I witnessed Natalie's Delta Delta Delta initiation or when I observed her bridesmaids on her wedding day. Blessings abounded in the friendships she had made.

Those New Jersey based bridezilla shows make the whole wedding look like a time of selfishness. Southern brides are ladies and therefore are treated as such. After all, as my mother said, it's the marriage that matters. It's not all about the wedding.

It's necessary to select dresses for your bridesmaids that complement each girl's figure. Have you ever seen a row of bridesmaids in strapless dresses seated in the pew? From the back, ~~they look naked~~ you see only shoulders. Just an observation.

And to mothers helping their daughters with strapless prom dresses and wedding gowns — If they constantly tug at the dresses, perhaps one with straps would be more becoming.

A note to brides:

Eight bridesmaids or less is a good number. Your sister(s), the groom's sister(s) if you are close, your childhood best friend and your closest friend should be included. Do not feel obligated to invite your six best friends from growing up. There is one who you stayed close to all through college and call when you go home to visit. Include her.

If you are asked to be in 18 weddings before you walk down the aisle, it is okay to slim down your own list. Many of the young wives/new mothers would enjoy being a guest just as much as being in the bridal party.

The Groom's Role and Groom's Cake

Good Southern boys ask their own daddy to be their best man. Then, out of respect for your fiancée-to-be's family, guys should always ask her daddy for her hand in marriage.

I love groom's cake. Why? Because nine times out of ten it is chocolate, of course. I'm one of those people who wants to have two slices of cake at the reception. The groom's cake is a Southern thing. Everyone remembers the red velvet armadillo from *Steel Magnolias*, but I've been to weddings where the groom loves pie. My son-in-law loves pineapple upside down cake, so that's what we had.

I've heard of serving groom's cake at the rehearsal dinner, which makes perfect sense to me. But I prefer it at the wedding reception, so I can always have a bite!

Groomsmen Guide

Do not let the groom be hung over on his wedding day.

Spit your gum out before ushering guests to their seats or while standing by your friend at the front of the church.

When giving the toast, don't assume your funny story will be entertaining to the guests. So, think first and maybe get a friend's take on what you'd like to share. Please don't mention former girlfriends of the groom. Be kind, show your fondness for your friend, and if you can pull off being humorous, go for it.

While serving as an usher, the woman is escorted up the aisle on his **left arm** with her husband and children following. The usher's right arm is reserved for escorting his bride down the aisle someday, after his own wedding ceremony.

Faux Pas
Or as I like to say, "Wedding Etiquette Gone Awry"

A Facebook announcement inviting people to a shower is gauche. It may work with younger people, but anyone older than 40 will consider this **tacky** and simply ignore it.

An e-vite, from the bride, inviting you to HER OWN shower is similarly improper. A paper invitation should be mailed and hostesses always should give the shower.

Flowers from Dollar General cut off and used as a boutonniere.

Plastic forks and plastic snap-together wine glasses at the reception should be avoided. They both break.

Having a "gift card" shower.
Why not put a stamped envelope in the invitation with a form?
___$50 ___$100 ___$200 check one
Charge to my Visa, Paypal, or Venmo
Thus, we can eliminate gifts entirely. (JOKING!)

I once was asked to address an envelope to myself at a wedding reception, assumably to make the bride's thank you note writing a little easier. She had my address to send me a wedding invitation. Was it that hard to look it up again? Besides that, I never received her note.

This is becoming a commonplace activity. I think it is common.

Never wear white to a wedding unless you are the bride.

It is her day. This rule is not antiquated. Don't be selfish. Let her be special. Yes, I am aware I mentioned this before. Please don't forget.

Prince Charles and Lady Diana were married in 1981 two weeks after Don and I married. I remember setting the alarm to watch the royal wedding. I've always been enthralled with her life and history.

I recently watched a special about the life of Princess Di. They showed a picture of Camilla Parker Bowles as a guest at the royal wedding. She was wearing white. I don't know the rules in the U.K., but I would assume it is super inappropriate for the prince's mistress to wear white. There possibly should have been some **hair pullin'** up in St. Paul's Cathedral that day!

If the bride wants her bridal party dressed in an all-white that is her choice. Same if she chooses for her bridesmaids to wear black. But, I must stress the role of the future mother-in-law, the groom's mother: Wear beige and keep your mouth shut.

If there is really such a thing as a Bridezilla, it is the mother's fault. A good mother never lets it get that far. Put a stop to inappropriate and spoiled behavior when she's young and you won't witness it when she is older.

A bit of wisdom to brides:

It is one thing to want lovely flowers adorning the church, have beautiful invitations with lined envelopes, or to have a fun (expensive) band for the reception. If it fits the budget, do what makes you happy. But ladies, the wedding is just one day... and marriage is a lifetime. Don't create a big bash where there is no foundation. You'll only feel let down when it's over.

Please do not applaud the soloist/music at a wedding. A wedding is a ceremony, not a performance.

Similarly, please refrain from applause at a funeral.

And it is not necessary to list the photographer or wedding planner in the program. It is your ceremony and you are not required to help them advertise.

Putting the Cart Before the Horse
Or as my son said as a child, "doing things backyards"

Celebrities are ruining everything. They get pregnant and have an elaborate wedding in Europe two years later with all the paparazzi.

Girls get pregnant and don't want to be cheated out of their wedding day. Well, their mamas should say, "Tough luck." But they don't.

I believe that huge formal weddings for second and third marriages as well as after a baby are gauche. Celebrities do it, but that doesn't make it right. We're forced to go along with it and act like it's no big deal.

Disagree if you'd like.

A couple in my community married after having two children and living together for quite some time, as well as having built a custom home. Don't get me wrong. I celebrate marriage. That's lovely to make a commitment. What wasn't lovely is that I got an invitation to her church shower the same day I got a wedding invitation. I'm sure several ladies in the congregation were not comfortable with this shower **sitch**. In fact, she had multiple showers and registered all around town (as printed on the invitations). Why didn't the bride's mother explain to her that some things are forfeited? The answer is because these young ladies don't want to hear it. They want what they see celebrities doing, and they want to be just like "normal" brides.

But their situation is not normal. Get married. Let close friends and family celebrate your union. Friends will send gifts if they are so inclined.

I do need to add that when it's your close friends, this is easier to accept, as weddings, big or small, should always be celebrated. In other words, I'm aware that I contradict myself. Oftentimes, grace is more important than tradition.

Tacky Wedding Plans I Have Witnessed First Hand or Been Told by Someone I Trust

The daughter from the first marriage dressed as a *mini-bride* and stood by her mother during the ceremony... like she was getting married, too.

The bride and her attendants wore bejeweled *flip-flops*. Down the aisle. Of the Church. This was not a destination beach wedding.

Brides wearing cowboy boots. Not my favorite. In Texas, yes.

Dogs as ring bearer? At a ranch, but not in the church, people. Please. Although I saw a wedding where the bridesmaids carried rescue puppies instead of bouquets. That's adorable.

Pulling an infant in a wagon, down the aisle.

"Will you marry me?' — written, with a *Sharpie, on the guy's stomach.*

Printed on bottom of wedding invitation:
No kids allowed
No spiky heels
(Don't wanna ruin the flo')

I'm not a fan of *eternity sand*. Do you really want to keep that for the rest of your life?

The wedding guest list being decided solely by the bride's side.

Receiving a *save the date card* from a couple, but never getting a wedding invitation.

I was asked once to print save the date cards for a couple that wasn't sending wedding invitations. I encouraged them to send an announcement. That's different.

If you are having a destination wedding and you are limited to who can be invited, it is appropriate for the parents of the couple to send a wedding announcement. This practice shares the good news while leaving the decision of giving a gift to the recipient.

Bride/Groom money jars to *vote who gets cake* in the face. My Mimi's reaction to that was, "Oh, me!

Who is Mimi?

Mimi was my friend for 30 years. She babysat our children as I worked at my store. She liked to tell people she raised me, too. In later years, I loved to take her with me to my Arkansas Parks & Tourism meetings. Everyone called her Mimi, even though her name was Janie. When I succeeded in visiting all 52 of our state parks we figured out she had seen 32 of them with me. She loved for me to post our exploits on Facebook!

She was Mimi to a host of children she impacted. She could make banana pudding, chicken & dumplings and chicken spaghetti like a BOSS! When I worked late hours, she'd feed my kids supper and have Don's and mine waiting on the counter in Tupperware. She spoiled us and loved us in spite of our faults.

Some of my favorite memories are of Mimi accompanying us to baseball tournaments and to plays. She absolutely loved to watch my children, as they were enthralled with the music, singing and acting. When Natalie and Josh had their babies, Mimi was in love once again, even though she had retired from childcare several years before. Mimi's daughter, Becky, graciously shared her with me. Oh, how blessed I was.

Back to *Caking* — The act of rubbing cake in your spouse's face. ~~Deplorable.~~ When did this become a thing? My precious mother-in-law requested that this be included in my book.

46

Apparently, she witnessed this activity and was mortified. Why would a couple have their guests watch such an embarrassing moment? Embrace the formality and respect this wedding tradition and share a bite. That is all. No smooshing allowed.

It is inappropriate for *another couple to announce their own engagement* or get engaged at a wedding they are attending. Don't steal the wedding couple's thunder. Similarly, pregnancy announcements and gender reveals by the newly married couple are highly unacceptable.

A friend was asked to help with a wedding. The bride's request: "We'll be getting married in a field and I'd like everyone to wear white. We're not going to have a ceremony – Just exchanging our VOWELS."

Mimi was invited to a wedding once with a new trend and she didn't know how to dress. The bride wore a traditional wedding gown. Her bridesmaids were in dresses. The groom wore a white shirt, jeans and cowboy boots. He and all of the groomsmen wore cowboy hats **up in the church house. Oh, Lordy.**

And the first time she saw burlap ribbon she said it looked **like a tow sack,** and couldn't imagine why brides were decorating with it!

Cindy's Faux Pas

Lest you think I'm perfect, let me share...
I never thought I'd be a wedding crasher, but I was. So, what happened? I had been on a weeklong beach vacation with friends. At the end of the week they were going to New Orleans for a wedding. I was totally happy with a quiet evening at the hotel. But when we arrived at the hotel, they announced that the bride's mother insisted I come. It wasn't a problem. Their husbands couldn't be there, so I was actually just filling in for one of them.

The ceremony was in the hotel's courtyard with a beautiful central fountain. It was a gloriously fun evening, complete with a second-line parade through the French Quarter.

And the highlight of the reception was when my friend Sheila, at age 60, got down and did the gator.

As I said, we had f.u.n.

I responded at home by sending a care package to the bride's mother. It included a note of thanks and several items to use for pampering after her months of creating such a wonderful event. Then I addressed an anniversary card to the couple, to be mailed in almost a year, thanking them for allowing me to enjoy their day, and letting them know I was the one in the coral dress they may have seen in their wedding pictures. No, I did not sign the guest book.

If you only read one chapter, please let it be this one.

Immediate family members don't give showers.
~~That is just plain tacky.~~

An aunt can host teas and luncheons, but don't let your sister host your shower. Since an invitation to a shower requires the attendee to bring a gift, it is simply incorrect for immediate family to be involved. Why? Because it crosses the line of soliciting gifts.

The mother, sisters and grandmothers shall never; I mean never-ever, host a party that asks for gifts. You should have a best friend who can host. The idea behind this is important to understand.

And the *bride should not plan her party* either. She is the guest of honor. She may have desires, but only express them if asked. The shower is given as a gift for her, not to her specifications. This comes up often when bridesmaids are planning a bachelorette weekend. The bride can suggest where she'd like to go, but the maid/matron of honor is in charge of planning according to the budgets and capabilities of the bridesmaids.

If your daughter is getting married, *every party should not be a shower.* Let your friends and family come together to celebrate the couple without having to bring a gift.

If you are only invited to ONE party for a bride, it should NOT be a shower. Coffees and teas introduce you to the bride, if needed, or to the mother/grandmother of the groom. My favorite party to host is a wine & cheese. My home adequately fits about 35 ladies for an early evening event of wine… and cheese. I throw in a few grapes and nuts, but the menu is pretty simple and it makes for a nice gathering.

Being invited to more than one shower for the same bride can be tacky. An exception to this is if it's your best friend's child — or different themes, possibly.

If you have given a party for a bride, you should not be asked to another party that includes giving a gift. (showers)

Best friends want to be invited, but others… not so much. So, if they gave a party, don't ask them to come to another party where they are expected to bring a gift.

Not being invited to the wedding, but being invited to a shower is just wrong. If you can't invite someone to your wedding, don't invite them to a gift-giving event. Period, end of story. If they choose to send you a wedding gift, they will. So, in other words, a bride's wedding guest list and shower lists should balance.

The conundrum has become, however, what to do when it's a destination wedding? Historically, the no wedding invitation/no shower invitation rule would make sense. That was before couples began getting married when they are older and choosing a destination venue instead of their home church. In this case, a bridal shower by friends is acceptable. But the MOB should make sure her friends understand why the guest list is smaller. Sending a post-wedding announcement is therefore appropriate. The truth is, dear friends want to celebrate the couple, whether they can attend or not.

Never request money or a gift card. It is simply NOT DONE as it exhibits entitlement. When an invitation is sent, it is not a gift request. It is an invitation to a gathering.

During Covid-19, people adjusted well. Virtual showers and drive-by birthday parades were creative and acceptable.

This section is a little complicated. Please read it again, and feel free to make notes in the margins.

Invitations

A lovely printed invitation, received by mail, will never go out of style. Do not send out a general announcement or copied flyer. Do not copy an invitation, or take a picture of it and text it to your friends. That's like saying, "You're not important enough to get the real invitation."

Offering to give a party involves a certain amount of financial commitment. If you cannot afford the financial or time commitment of giving a party, simply send a nice gift. Each party does not need to have a dozen hostesses.

But if giving a party, invest in the gift from the hostesses, the invitations, centerpiece, and make sure the food is delicious. It's very frustrating for me to give a party with a limited budget and have to adjust plans in order to save money. I'm not referring to extravagance; I just don't want to be cheap.

The hostess having the party in her home sets the tone for the type of party (shower, coffee, tea, wine & cheese) and the level of dressiness. She decides if she's comfortable using her sterling silver or pottery to serve. The less she has to borrow the easier it is for everyone involved.

I enjoy this concept for parties with multiple hostesses: If it's in your home, you are not responsible for the food preparation.

Hostesses should expect the event to cost more if it is at a venue. The rental is worthwhile if your group doesn't have time to prepare a home or if more space is needed.

You are not expected to invite your co-workers to your wedding. Your professional life and private life have some barriers that are not often crossed. Your employer may have a policy of having small inner-office showers for brides and expectant mothers. However, only your very close friends expect to be invited.

How to address invitations and correspondence:
Mr. and Mrs. Don M. Smith
Mrs. Don Smith if I were a widow
Or, Mrs. Cindy Smith

Ms. Cindy Smith if I were divorced
Miss Cindy Chandler if I had never married

If a woman does not want to be recognized by her marital status, she may choose Ms. This is especially prevalent in the business world.

When listing hosts and hostesses on an invitation, it should read: *Cindy & Don Smith*, as the man's first name is never separated from his last name.

Obviously, the wedding invitations have a couple of rules:

The names on the inner envelope signify who is specifically invited. Please note: If your children's names aren't listed, or it doesn't say plus one, **don't** bring your kids or a date.

Never assume you can bring a friend, since guests are not encouraged to bring their own guests. Seating in the church is limited, most importantly to people who actually KNOW the couple getting married. Food at receptions costs money, often LOTS of it.

Calling off the Wedding

When is it okay to call off a wedding? Any time. Don't marry if you're not positive.

A ceremony with a pastor presiding is a Covenant with God. Don't go through with it to avoid embarrassment or because so much time and money has been committed.

There are, however, two simple rules:

1. Return all gifts. Not to the store so the burden is on them. Return the gifts to those who sent them, with a simple note. There is absolutely no excuse for not doing this.
Another option is to send a gift card in the amount of the gift with the note. A sample note could read, "As you may know, we have cancelled/postponed our wedding. Your thoughtful gift means so much, we felt it should be returned to you."

Close friends may insist you keep the gift, knowing the difficulty of the situation. But the option is theirs.

2. If he breaks the engagement, the bride keeps the ring, as it was a gift. If the bride breaks the engagement, she must return the ring.

Please teach your children to marry out of love for their partners. The saying is, "If you marry for money you'll earn every penny."

And, "It's better to wait long than marry wrong."

And tell your children, "Remember, you marry the family."

Divorce

I don't have a whole lot to say about divorce except it is sad. To some it is a necessity.

Make an effort to co-parent with your ex for the benefit of the children, because they will carry the burden forever. I love stories of when one parent takes the children shopping for a birthday gift for the other parent after divorce. It's just healthy, y'all.

But to be honest, I wouldn't have been good in divorce. I basically told Don if he fell in love with someone else he'd better hope she really loved him. Because I wouldn't go to prison for murder, but I'd probably shoot him in the knees and she'd have to push him around in his wheelchair. And when he came home, all his belongings would be in a big pile in the front yard, on fire. I'd probably sell all his guns for $25 each, too.

We're still together.

Gift Registry thoughts:

Gift (noun)
A thing given willingly to someone without payment; a present

Gift registries were developed so a couple could receive matching china and flatware. Somehow the concept morphed into a wish list. I made a lot of money at the Periwinkle Place helping couples receive gifts they liked and my customers being satisfied with their selection.

Apparently, many couples now think that a gift registry is a way to get exactly **what they want**. Y'all, it isn't a required gift list. This attitude just comes off as entitlement to me.

Mothers, please remind your daughters about gratitude. And being humble.

A gift is a choice. If I want to shower the bride with my favorite cookbook, or a pan to fry bacon, it has meaning behind it, and shouldn't be viewed as an unkind or thoughtless act. Moreover, brides whose mothers consistently gave $20 shower gifts shouldn't be surprised when the $100 gifts they hoped for never arrive.

I've even read a Facebook post where the bride compared the cost of a meal at her reception to what she expects her guests to spend on a gift for the couple. Where is her grandmother, ready to **jerk a knot in her**? I am a generous gift giver. I just like to have a little leeway so that my gifts stand out. Don't get me wrong. Gift registries are necessary, easy, and all the norm. But if you find an antique cake server, go ahead and give the couple something they never considered they wanted.

Resist to List

The absolute worst concept is listing where a bride or expectant mother is registered ON the invitation.
Even the tiniest suggestion of a registry (a note, link, anything) smacks of greed and poor manners. As many Southern mamas and grandmothers will tell you, it is tacky. Let that sink in.

It may be helpful, but with a simple phone call to the mother, or realizing every bride loves Pottery Barn and Target, you can find a place to shop. If you want to buy the couple a piece from their china pattern, it's pretty easy to guess which department store or specialty gift shop is handling it. My grandmothers would have fallen over if they had received a shower invitation with a list of WHERE TO SHOP right on the invitation. I absolutely must lead a revolution to stop this. My goodness.

Once I received the registry notice inserted with the wedding invitation.

A new, perfectly acceptable process is the website for the bride and groom. Information about the wedding weekend and the couple's registry can be found there. Let that be enough change, please.

You've seen it before, but now that you are aware, let friends know that it is inappropriate to print registry info on the shower invitations.

Registering does not extend to graduation announcements. The high school rite of passage involves gifts, so call the parent if you need a suggestion. Sending a check is always appreciated.

Unless your parents are CLOSE FAMILY FRIENDS, classmates in the same graduating class do NOT exchange gifts.

Couples should be counseled to never consider having a honeymoon fund. For goodness sake, you are not "owed" a trip simply by committing your life to another. If you have a honeymoon fund, you are essentially asking for money, which is crass and an embarrassment something to avoid. It has become popular enough that it is called a *Honey-fund*.

Again: Just because someone else does it, doesn't make it right. And I heard of a couple building a house who established a website so friends and family could "buy a door." NO, just no.

I recently saw a "Stuff the Wallet" shower invitation. They should be ashamed.

Once I gave a monetary gift to a truly special couple in my life. I encouraged them to use it for an experience on their honeymoon. I gave it by choice and received a kind note telling me about it. That's different.

Now, many younger people say, "We already have everything. What's wrong with asking for money?" Just simply reread what's written above.

Money dances?

Seriously. We just don't have those in the South.
Isn't that reserved for strippers?

I've heard that in some places it is customary to pin a dollar bill to your lapel on your birthday, then others will give you money. I would give a dollar to a child, just as I pull over for every single lemonade stand. But if an adult did this, I would just ignore it.

Gift Bags and Transportation for Hotel Wedding Guests

These are not a necessity, but are certainly appreciated. They can include local brochures about things to do, local favorites, a couple of snacks, water, pain reliever, etc. It's fine to team up with the groom's family to create the bags.

Including a schedule of events is also helpful. It is nice to provide transportation for the guests from the hotel to the wedding venue and/or church to the reception if you are financially able. Remember, transportation for the wedding party is, however, a necessary kindness.

For Natalie's wedding, the limousine driver took her special "church lady friends" to our house for the reception, while the wedding party was having post-ceremony photos taken. Then he came back to transport the bridesmaids, then lastly, the newly betrothed couple.

Wedding Favors

Traditionally, a piece of the wedding cake is boxed for guests to take home. Wedding favors are optional, but thoughtful. We gave wooden spoons that had a heart-shaped bowl.

I've seen candy "bars", flower seeds, and small bottles of local sauces given as favors. Guests enjoy a surprise, so if you'd like, include favors.

Shopping for the Dress

These are guidelines to follow no matter where you live. But a kind Southern gal would always plan to be patient and courteous. She learns at an early age that this pays off.

Number one:

Make an appointment. Don't just arrive at the store/boutique and expect exceptional service.

Number two:

Shop early to allow time for delivery and for alterations. When you see brides with their dresses bustled to dance at the reception that is not included with the dress. You must hire an alterations person to sew those **riggin's** into your gown. And it's a good idea to ask your maid/matron of honor to practice so you're not tied up (no pun intended) when you could be dancin'.

Number three:

Be candid about your price range. You want to be treated well regardless of what you can spend. Independent boutiques will give you the best customer service and won't be as commission-based. The chains, however, will have more regular sales. Don't overspend and regret damaging the budget you've planned. I've complimented many brides who shared that their dresses were not expensive, and I would've never known. A lady is never so beautiful as on her wedding day.

Number four:

Have an idea as to style, fabric and beading, but be willing to listen and learn. Don't be **dead set** on a style, because another may be more flattering to your figure. The dress also needs to be appropriate as to the location... beach vs. cathedral.

Number five:

Don't bring your entourage. Invite your mother, and your sister, or your best friend. It's nice to include a grandmother, and if the mother-of-the-groom has only sons, she would probably be very pleased to be included. *It is not your bridal party's job to select your wedding dress.* In fact, they could easily be a distraction. If you want to share the excitement with your bridesmaids, meet them later, for drinks.

Number six:

Wear pretty undergarments... not a sports bra... for your fittings. I don't care if you wear a thong, but you may want to wear more traditional panties that day, or your Spanx.

Number seven:

Sit in your dress at your fitting. I know you want to look thin and beautiful on your wedding day, but comfort is important!

Advice to the Couple

Make sure you eat at your reception. Whereas Yankee receptions tend to be sit-down affairs with a formal dinner, we Southerners often enjoy delicious buffets, or food stations, to allow for staggered eating and more guests. Have food to-go packed to take when you leave your reception, or take the time to eat a bite in a private area before you get too caught up in the festivities.

A note to the groom: It's smart to plan an extra day after the wedding before leaving to go on your honeymoon. Enjoy an evening or two in a local hotel to get rested before your travels begin.

You'll go to bed angry at some point in your marriage. Who are we kidding? And one of you will snore. And he may go bald and you may gain weight. So, learn to laugh and to forgive. And remember what attracted you to one another.

If Daddy Don and I are in a fast food restaurant and he goes to the restroom before we leave, when he walks out, my heart still leaps. I know that sounds ridiculous, but it does. I hope you have that.

Thank You Notes

The rule of having a year to write one is false. That's all. Someone once said it and everyone wanted to believe it, but who really wants to wait a year for a note? How sincere can it be? What IS true is that it is appropriate to GIVE a gift up to a year after the wedding. Three months is better. But, who's gonna ever turn down a gift? It's never too late to give a gift.

My brothers and I spent a little bit of time after each Christmas and birthday writing notes to our grandparents. We could either mope and whine, or get them done. It wasn't so bad. It morphed into a love of note writing for me and added much to my relationship with them until their passing away while I was a young adult.

When Natalie had her twins, she managed to breastfeed the babies and write all of her thank you notes before going back to work at ten weeks. She's exceptional though, and comes from a long line of gifted note writers.

Taylor, on the other hand, hated writing thank you notes when he graduated from high school. I believe this to be true for all guys. But I taught him how to describe his use for the gift, and include a memory of his relationship with the giver in his notes. Before long he was critiquing the notes I was receiving from his classmates.

There are many who say, "What's the need for a note if you thank the person when you open it?" There is validity to that, but then again, what do you have to lose if you take a minute to tell the person how much the gift means to you and how much you care for them? Reflect on your friendship or family memories and put a smile on their face. After all, they took time and spent money to show you that they care.

When you think about it, a well-written thank you note will be appreciated longer than you'll remember the gift.

And for any formal correspondence, please use black ink. Using hearts to dot your i's and cutesy colored pens is for teenagers.

Entertaining

R.S.V.P
Repondez s'il vous plait

This is French for, "please reply." It does not mean *at the last minute* or *only if you cannot come*. It means, contact the hostess and tell her you received the invitation and are looking forward to the event OR that you unfortunately cannot attend. An RSVP allows the hostess to plan the amount of food, beverages, and seating. This cannot be done last minute, so if she hears from everyone in a timely manner the details can be set. It is rude to not reply.

When sending an invitation, remember "Please R.S.V.P." is redundant.

Reply as requested: by text, email or note.

To any formal invitation, a response "in kind" is expected. That means if Mr. and Mrs. Don Smith cannot attend a wedding, my note should say, "Mr. and Mrs. Don Smith decline with regret the invitation of March 26." You have an obligation to respond whether or not a response card is included.

Accept with pleasure or regretfully decline, and you need not give a reason why. (However, my daughter and I loved the short notes on her wedding RSVPs.)

Inserts with wedding invitations can include:

    a separate invitation to the reception
    a detailed map
    a response card (with an addressed and stamped

envelope). I especially liked one that said, "You can expect to see us up dancing when we hear: _____"

What should they NEVER include? You got it — gift registry preference. Good job!

Why the inner envelope on a wedding invitation? It dates back to when the mail was delivered by horseback. The inner envelope prevented the invitation from being soiled. No longer a necessity, but the tradition continues to use both envelopes with a wedding invitation.

Also, the inner envelope lists who, specifically, is invited. Please note if your children are included, or not.

I also learned this: On wedding invitations, "request the honour of your presence" is only used if the ceremony is taking place in a house of worship. For a civil ceremony, one not being held in a place of worship, and for an invitation to the reception only, correcting wording is: "request the pleasure of your company."

Save-the-Date cards enable guests from out-of-town to reserve hotel rooms. 2020 brought us something new: Change-the-Date cards. **Bless their hearts**.

Hand address the invitations, even if hiring a calligrapher is not in the budget. The no-no here is a printed *label*. It is okay, however, to print the entire envelope using a calligraphy font and a printer.

Everyone over age eighteen gets his or her own invitation, even if they still live at home.

What about the "*plus one*?" This is not a requirement for every single person invited to the wedding. If they are engaged, yes. If they are living together, yes. Otherwise, not everyone who is dating or wants to bring a date is automatically given this option.

Regrets

This means when you get any invitation and look at your calendar, if you have plans that conflict, let the hostess know right away. Otherwise, she can assume you'll be there. Letting her know at the last minute that ~~better things came up~~ you have a conflict is impolite.

Babies and Baby Showers

Baby showers with more than 60 guests are tacky. Your girlfriends should give baby showers. Many older generation ladies prefer to send gifts when the baby arrives. An exception would be your mother's closest friends. But really, keep it small.

Some "Don'ts" and "Oh no, you didn't!"

Baby showers for babies number two, three, and four are improper. Do I need to repeat that? Yes, they are improper. Your first shower was to help you get the essentials. By baby number two you are on your own. You are seasoned parents. Grow up. Your friends may choose to have a luncheon to honor you, but please don't accept an offer of a shower.

When you have subsequent babies, your friends and loved ones will give you a gift — clothing, something personalized. I received more gifts at home after Taylor was born, with no shower. With the birth of a second baby, you already have a high chair, infant seat, baby bathtub, etc.

A friend got an invitation to an acquaintance's fourth baby shower. Printed on the invitation it said, "Because the couple has everything, gift cards would be appreciated." Really?

I touched on this subject earlier, but humor me and keep reading.

60

I think the younger generation (and I swore I wasn't going to use that phrase) thinks they won't get a gift if it's not a shower...so **by damn**, let's have another shower. Or, because one friend had two showers, then everyone deserves the same treatment... even if it's your third birth. #giftgrab #entitledmaybe.

It's not true, so relax.

Enjoy having that second baby and witness that friends will bring gifts and delicious meals, too. I have had numerous people ask me about this rule. The young mothers say, "Oh, I couldn't tell people no." Oh, yes you can. Thank them for the kind gesture and tell them you don't need another shower. If your mama knew the rule, she would tell you. So, let's say it's not your fault. She is at fault for not teaching you that you DO NOT HAVE MORE THAN ONE SHOWER. Mothers, please raise your daughters without the expectation of showers with each birth.

Now we'll get even deeper into "stepping on toes" — I am personally uncomfortable with baby showers for unwed mothers. Call me a prude, but I have trouble having the same celebration party for the birth of a child who has unwed parents. I know it is commonplace and I should be more accustomed to this, but I'm not. Certain things are to be celebrated and some things should be handled more discretely.

I celebrate parenthood and always gift the baby when born, but I am not comfortable hosting a shower when the couple has no commitment. I know a young mother needs help, and that is where her family should be involved.

Don't be a hater. My intent is to preserve the Southern way of doing things. You are welcome to disagree. But people are watching. And just because it is done does not make it correct behavior. Ladies much older than me are appalled when asked to attend these showers.

<u>About modern birth.</u>

When I was born, my father was in the waiting room. When my children were born, my husband stood at my head, encouraging me (...except for that one time he said he was "so tired!"). Now, apparently the delivery room is more relaxed. Some girls want their mommas with them. Doesn't this take away the intimacy of the little family? I love the way hospitals include the father more, now, with having him put the baby's footprint on his scrub shirt.

Either way, I actually have a photo on my phone, poached from Facebook, of a new mother, legs splayed, holding her newborn, and the afterbirth shows in the picture. I was aghast. But I saved it, to show my BFF, and I don't mind telling y'all, right now, to keep some things PRIVATE! Stirrups just are not photo appropriate.

A *"Sprinkle"* is a little celebration. When I had my second child several of us were due at the same time. A few friends had a small luncheon in our honor and gave us each a new nightgown. That was so thoughtful. I've heard of some girls stocking their friends' freezers with casseroles. Co-workers giving diapers is nice. But really, one shower is it. Believe me.

And a "Grandma Shower?" We grandmothers can afford to buy a pack & play or a booster seat for a new grandchild to use at our home. We can pull out the vintage toys. Please don't let this become a thing, because it is ridiculous. I can take a pretty burp cloth and a "grandmother" storybook to my friend because I choose to, but please no showers.

One of the perks of giving birth is the delicious food your friends and church family will bring to you and your husband. The hospital may release you the very next day, but at least you'll be pampered with meals. My friend, Sheri, brought such delicious meals that I actually considered having a third child!

But let me tell you, there wouldn't have been another shower. And again, leave where the expectant mother is registered OFF of the invitation. A simple phone call can give you the answer.

The Sip 'n See

This little gathering is given by friends of the grandmother.

The new mother is invited back to her hometown so friends can meet her baby. This is by no means a shower. (Any gifts can be delivered to the home prior to the party.) Guests are invited for an afternoon to meet the baby and visit with the mother and grandmother, and if you are lucky, the great-grandmother. There is no need to have a sip 'n see in the town where the young family lives.

Southern infants typically are dressed in pastels. They are young such a short time, so we avoid the bold color palette. If your northern friends dress their little girls in ~~garish~~ red dresses on their first Christmas, that is their choice. The word newborn and "red corduroy" should never be spoken in the same sentence. A Southern Belle will assure her infant daughter will wear a white or cream smocked dress every time. Southern baby boys often wear "aprons". The daddies don't like them, but it sure makes diaper changes go more smoothly. They've got a lifetime to wear blue jeans. In the past, the benefit of infants wearing gowns was that they couldn't crawl into the hearth.

Similarly, now it's very difficult to buckle a gown-wearing infant into a car seat!

Southerners love double names: Anna Claire, Mary Stewart, Mary Alice, John Arthur, Thomas Clark, and Mae Louise.

We also like using old family (last) names as first names. Grandmère's maiden name was Taylor. Taylor's best friend just named his daughter Collins Reese. Collins is Garrett's wife's maiden name. We like tradition, and we **love us** some monograms.

Part Three
More About Me, Because, this is Sort Of a Memoir

What makes me "Not a Southerner"?

1. I was not born South of the Mason-Dixon Line.

That's a biggie, but bear with me. I've done a lot of observation and assimilation. Thus, the book's title, *Southern As I See It*

2. I've never grown a successful vegetable garden. Last year I worked in the Boys & Girls Club Learning Garden, but I had lots of help. And I'll admit, the weeds got the best of me. I have a lovely boxwood fenced herb garden, and grow cherry tomatoes and peppers in pots. But, that's all. I love referring to it as a kitchen garden (or *potager*). I think it makes me sound sophisticated AND may convince new acquaintances that I can actually cook.

3. I don't make good gravy.

One of the most satisfying parts about writing this book (besides sitting on the porch at our lake house) has been finding truly Southern words and phrases. Some have made me laugh, and others just make me love the South even more. I'll hear a phrase in conversation and think "Oh! There's a good one." I cannot wait to share my interpretation of **Southern Speak** in Part IV.

The only thing that truly makes me "clam up" is karaoke. I really cannot sing. I love the Lord and at least TRY in church (I'm SO much better when Alicia is there!), but you will never see me up on stage singing. Dancing? Yes. Lots of people are bad singers, drink too much, and have so much fun singing anyhow, but I JUST CAN'T DO IT.

I'm pretty willing to do anything else, like walk into a room of strangers and strike up a conversation. I like to talk to just about everyone. I love to hear their stories. Especially wait staff and cab drivers. I talk to people in line at the post office and checking out at the grocery store. I like to laugh. It just makes my day good.

I had my own 60th Birthday Party. Now, to be honest, I let Daddy Don pay for it, but I planned it myself. And nearly 80 people came to the Hotel Monteleone in New Orleans. We had a reception, and a Second Line Parade, and when I'm in the nursing home I'll still be giggling about how fun it was.

Photo by Curtis W. Chandler

It took me 60 years to figure out that I like yoga. And I love riding a bicycle. Other forms of exercise; not so much. A few years back my friend Weston and I tried mountain biking. I survived, but that activity is checked off the list. That, and zip lining. Once was enough.

This self-checkout at the grocery store works against me having time to visit. Also, I don't work at Target, so why would I want to use self-check? Oh, and recently I got cash back...only I forgot to get it. I guess I blessed someone that day.

Don, is not a talker except in close company. He's reflective and tends to keep his thoughts to himself. When he does share something, it is often witty. I pretty much get on his nerves. When watching me talk, he tends to grin and shake his head a lot. Sometimes up and down, mostly side to side...in disbelief. He won't want me telling his private business, so I'll keep it brief. He was the boy across the street. I fell in love with him at Sigma Chi Derby Days when I was eighteen, and he didn't have a chance. He tells people nowadays it's considered stalking.

I sometimes get ~~angry as hell~~ irritated with him, but he's such a good guy. When I point out the things he does that get on my nerves he says, "It's those minor imperfections that kept me from getting a better wife." Most of my friends think he should get an award for putting up with me. He takes the other side in discussions just to make it fair.

He's scary smart. He's good as giving me the brief and uncomplicated version of whatever is going on in the news, because I sometimes don't want the depression of watching the news when I can watch a good movie. He was and is a good daddy. And he loves those grandkids.

My dad, Bill, was affectionate. He loved food that wasn't good for him, so Mom couldn't trust him to go to the grocery store. He enjoyed being a scoutmaster, flying small planes, and family camping vacations. He confidently walked to the front of the church every Sunday, and he sang loudly. I'm ashamed of my junior high self for ever being embarrassed.

My mother, Joyce, loved to read in her hammock, study the Bible, play the piano, and she taught herself to play the banjo. She was a wonderful artist — in every medium from watercolor, to weaving, to oil and acrylic, to enameling. She even did macramé the first time it was popular.

My parents believed in education above all else. Mom went to Wellesley and my Dad went to M.I.T. I didn't have my own television, stereo, or car. I had access to them, but never "my own." However, I was always promised a college education, something they were able to provide for all three of us. In fact, all of my grandparents were college graduates in the 1920s and 1930s. My honest and kind Southern father-in-law earned his bachelor's degree and law degree simultaneously. Pretty impressive.

Mom didn't make us do chores. She was a college graduate, but a 60s/70s housewife. She did the cooking, cleaning and carpooling and we were required to keep our rooms straight and be pleasant to be around. I guess she kept her sanity by having morning coffee with our neighbors, enjoying her book club, and being active in church and other organizations. They didn't have "Mother's Day Out" back then. She just sent us outside to play. Out of respect, I set the table every evening as Mom and I caught up on the day. I guess my brothers helped as well. They probably mowed and took the trash out. For the most part I remember everything always being clean and straight and organized.

She never complained or griped at us. She picked up after us, cooked three meals a day, and baked a weekly batch of chocolate chip cookies. We went to church on Sundays. She taught me to knit when I was five. She sewed nearly all of my clothes until I graduated from high school. And they were outfits I was definitely proud to wear. We spent hours and hours together selecting patterns and fabric. When I came home from school, the dress or outfit would be completed and displayed with pride on my bed. I never see a bolt of fabric or Vogue pattern without thinking of her.

I was not so gracious with my own children. I was often impatient and frustrated with housework. I was a working mother who married an old-fashioned Southern gentleman. Working around the house and helping to clean never occurred to him after long days in the field. The responsibilities of owning my store kept me busy. After a few years we hired a weekly housekeeper. My children didn't really like having "jobs" but didn't complain too much. They both keep tidy homes now.

I was a good kid. I never wanted to "disappoint" my parents. That's not to say I never got in trouble, but I never was the "sneak out my window" kind of girl. Working with the youth at our church for more than 10 years, I think the kids were always a little disappointed I didn't have better stories to tell. My friends and I hid in the trunk of the car to get into the drive-in movie. Once we jumped the fence to swim in the public pool. That's about it.

I did, however, steal my older brother's coin collection when I was about seven. I spent it at the candy store up the street. Yes, I got a **whuppin'**.

Joyceisms:

Things I learned from my mother

(Note: My mother is in her eleventh year of dementia now; my prayers to anyone going through this heartache. And as Jenna Bush said, I am now the keeper of her memories.)

Spend your money on the trip, not on your wardrobe.

It's your job to be kind and make good grades. Leave the rest to your father and me.

Don't hesitate to apologize. It will stop a conflict. Even if you feel you're not at fault, apologize. Something is wrong that you can fix.

I've heard it said this way: Apologizing does not always mean that you're wrong and the other person is right. It just means that you value your relationship more than your ego.

Put the top sheet on upside down when making the bed. That way the pretty part shows when you fold it back.

If you are choking on water, lift your arms above your head. (This really works. I guess it opens up the rib cage.)

Everything in moderation. I wish I followed this as far as food is concerned. Why does it taste so good?

Never congratulate a bride. On the card, put "Best Wishes!" and in person tell her how happy you are for her. Congratulating a bride insinuates that you cannot believe she finally landed a husband.

Never buy anything you cannot afford to pay for at time of purchase. (Or pay the credit card bill **in full** each month.)

You're never too old to learn.

Things I remember her saying:

"*Not on the Orientals!*" (She was very protective of her antique rugs.)

"Don't use the good scissors for that." (She was also very protective of her sewing scissors.)

Some Random Thoughts:

I took my children to productions at the children's theater when they were little. I love cultural experiences including art museums, plays, ballets, concerts, and history. (Although, I don't recall ever going to the opera.) I didn't want them to grow up lacking confidence from not having been exposed to the Arts. Taylor didn't want to go to the ballet but enjoyed it once he got there. As he got older, he recognized the athleticism in ballet. My Mimi said I made everything a learning experience.

Of all things, I love to knit baby hats. I crochet dishrags, too. They're not complicated, or difficult, so I do a few each month just to give away. Anything made with love is a pleasure, but becomes a job if you intend to sell it.

When I first moved to the South I became acquainted with small town newspapers. I loved the columns by local ladies that told "who visited whom" in the past week. They always ended with, "and a good time was had by all."

I learned to fly in high school. My dad always liked to fly, so most of our family vacations centered around camping, swimming, and Dad getting to fly gliders. So, when he offered to pay for my lessons, I jumped at the chance. I learned to fly back before GPS was there to help, I soloed, I passed the written exam, but you know what? I never got my license because I was TOO SHY to communicate with the control tower. WHAT? And in college, I waited until my senior year to take freshman speech because I was petrified to speak in front of a group.

I made it though... and for the last eleven years I loved being invited to speak about The Natural State. I was blessed to be a commissioner for Arkansas Parks and Tourism. You never know where life will take you.

It's important to find your passion...to find your happiness. It doesn't come from another person. It comes from enjoying the passage of time. (See: The Secret 'O Life by James

Taylor) What does that mean? It means live with no regrets and enjoy. Open your heart. Don't hold on. Just enjoy the ride.

I oftentimes say **a whole nother** as if another is two words. Example, "I got over my cold, but coughed for a whole nother week." I'm quite sure this is Southern slang as my computer tries to autocorrect as I am typing.

I have lived by this adage for several years:
The older I get the less time I have to do things I didn't want to do in the first place. Say yes to the things that inspire and interest you, and decline those that don't. But make the world a better place.

I didn't learn "righty tighty, lefty Lucy" until my thirties. I didn't know that the "short bus" was for special-needs children, because I always saw the cheerleaders riding in it. I've never done a cartwheel or ridden on a motorcycle.

Befriend the school secretary. She does a lot to hold the school together and will be a big help while your kids are going through school. Remember her birthday, and Christmas, and Administrative Professionals Day.

Once I was trying to demonstrate how to do the relay race at one of Taylor's birthday parties. You know... kick the ball, go down the slide, jump over the box... oops! I caught my toe and landed on my buttock in front of all the kids. Too bad this was pre- Funniest Home Videos, or I would have won $10,000.

Don't learn to do things you don't really want to do. I never kept the baseball book or made popcorn in the concession stand. But I was good at taking orders and making change! I pretend I don't know how to use the grill, too.

I cannot be trusted to buy canned frosting. I know if it's in my pantry, and am not satisfied until I eat it... all. Yes, I'm weak.

I'm not competitive in sports. I can definitely still have a good time if our team loses. Taylor was fiercely competitive, keeping score at age five even when they were playing "for fun." I played tennis for several years (until my skirt got too tight). My older friend, Bonnye Jean, would always call to ask how we did. Oftentimes I had to tell her, "We lost... but we looked good!"

I am deathly afraid of snakes, y'all. I mean, if I see one I have to go get back under my covers in the bed. Doesn't matter if it's a big snake, a small snake, or just a stick that looks like a snake. I respect other's phobias. My friend Amanda had to sit down at the base of the Empire State Building because the thought of going up that high made her weak. I've been to the top of the Burj Khalifa, so I'm good on heights.

I love community service. I get satisfaction from being given a task and bringing the project to fruition. The satisfaction is all the recognition I need.

I read something years ago that was life changing for me: There are some people who go through life seizing whatever they can for themselves. Then there are others who, once their lives are touched, cannot help but leave others changed as well. I hope that's me.

As for raising kids, y'all, the concept of a super-mom is a myth. It's impossible to do everything well, although we all really try. I like things picked up and for the house to be decorated for every holiday or season. I love working in my yard — planting, trimming and growing flowers to cut and share, or bring inside. I gave great birthday parties for my kids. I like to entertain and to give beautiful gifts. But, my weekly housekeeper is very much appreciated for keeping things clean underneath. We have dogs and live next to a huge field of either cotton, soybeans or corn. We have a lot of dust. It's endless.

I love my husband's cousin's wife, Nan. (For short, we just tell everyone that we're cousins.) When she was in the throes of raising three sons she just put up most of her decor. She simply didn't want to dust it. And after a few years she got rid of most of it because she hadn't missed it. Her minimalist attitude is intriguing, but something I'll admit I could never do. My stuff makes me happy. It's an expression of my life. I pass things along, but I have some favorites that make our home ours. However, let's say a little prayer for my kids, who, when I die will have to figure out what to do with it!

I am lucky that Don is easy. He doesn't care if we eat Subway or if we go out to eat. He's pleased if I actually make a meal. Thank goodness. But, he only likes leftovers once!

Back to the topic of the supermom ... ladies, give up something. And give yourselves a break. Whether you hire having your yard trimmed, your kids' birthday cakes baked, or your presents wrapped, don't do it all or you may collapse. Some moms have piles of laundry or need help with the dishes. If you're stressed, take a bunch of shirts to the dry cleaners. It's more important that you enjoy your family than to waste a day ironing.

Modern husbands pick up the slack. In fact, my daughter is artsy and my son-in-law likes everything straight, so they have good teamwork.

One year on Mother's Day afternoon I was pulling weeds in our front yard, grateful that my kids were old enough to go inside and get their own snacks. Don came out later to check on me. We started talking about if we were doing things right — balancing work, kids, church, finances — basically, were ~~they getting screwed up~~ we doing a good job? I was so touched that he asked… and I was busy weighing things out … when he said, "Y'know, we can sell your car, move out to the (hunting) camp house. You can sell your store, the kids can take the bus to school, you can raise a little vegetable garden and really simplify…" I thought about it. And then I said, "No, we're good!"

I got a message from God when my children were young. I believe Taylor was not yet one, so Natalie was three. I was trying to smock and sew Christmas outfits for them. Combine that with long hours in my gift shop during the holidays, and I was **having a come-apart**. I heard The Lord, loudly and clearly, guide me to put my sewing machine away and start buying my children's clothes.

Big projects can be satisfying, but not at the expense of my family. I often get involved in community projects, church committees or something or another, and get stressed. That's when Daddy Don says, "You brought it on yourself." Balance is hard, y'all.

A friend kept asking me several years ago to attend early morning meetings to "strategize" ways to improve our small town. I don't do mornings well. That is unless you're talking about 10 a.m. I finally explained to him that the smartest thing I could do was to raise my two kids the best I could, and then we'd see. And what do you know? Our kids turned out great …now I work tirelessly to help our community. But I still don't do early morning meetings.

> If you want to
> change the world,
> go home and love
> your family.
> – Mother Theresa

Quotes I love:

It's not how you live in the South but how the South lives in you.

In the South, please and thank you are magical words and Ma'am and Sir know no age.

It's called a twang. Accents are for Yankees.

Say what you will about the South, but nobody retires and moves up North.

A rising tide lifts all boats.

The spirit never ages. — Isabel Allende

The real test of good manners is to put up with bad manners pleasantly.

Blessed are those who can give without remembering and take without forgetting.

Fashion is what you buy. Style is what you do with it.

There is no weakness in forgiveness.

You cannot argue with ignorance — you can only forgive it.

The most meaningful charity is anonymous.

Be the woman who fixes another woman's crown, without telling the world that it was crooked.

Dead people receive more flowers than the living ones because regret is stronger than gratitude.
— *Anne Frank*

Done right, done once. — *Greek saying*

Weak people seek revenge.
Strong people forgive.
Intelligent people ignore.

The only person you should try to be better than is the person you were yesterday.

The purpose of life is not to be happy. It is to be useful, to be honorable, to be compassionate, to have it make some difference that you have lived and lived well.
— *Ralph Waldo Emerson*

... And anything by Dolly Parton. Y'all, she's wise.
If you don't like the road you're walking, start paving another one.
We cannot direct the wind, but we can adjust the sails.
Don't get so busy making a living that you forget to make a life.
Sometimes great hair is the best revenge.

... And a good rule I live by:
Always keep champagne handy in the refrigerator and ice cream in the freezer.

And store poster board paper between your mattress and box springs. You'll always have some, and it won't be tattered.
You're welcome for that little gem.

What Makes Don Happy

Solitude
A night at the camp sleeping under the tin roof while it's raining
Hunting with our son
Visits from his children and grandchildren
A good harvest
Being invited to a crawfish boil
A good summer rain on the farm
Going to the horse races
Finding Native American artifacts on the farm (He has over 200 arrowheads.)
Cut up watermelon, ready to eat, in the refrigerator
Wait. Am I on this list?

What Makes Me Happy

When my kids and grandkids are home
Galavantin' — I absolutely love to travel, experience new things, visit with new people, and embrace their culture
Entertaining at home/or being entertained
Days when both my yard is mowed and my home is clean. It's hard to achieve.
Tulips and daffodils blooming in the Spring
The sounds and "feels" at the beach/finding seashells
Browsing in a bookstore
Riding with Don in the car, where I have his undivided attention, even if he gets to pick the music
My Church Family
The voices of children singing

My Village

The Cube:
     I have a group of girlfriends who came together because of the shared friendship of our husbands. They were all Sigma Chis at the University of Arkansas. We girls knew one another, but truly reunited when our kids started college and we began

tailgating together. Our husbands had gotten together semi-annually for years at the deer camp. But we women were busy raising our kids, so at the time our kids went to college we were open to new friendships. There are seven of us and we live in different cities. I know, a cube has six sides, but the name has meaning to us.

There are two second wives in the Cube, but we closed the Second Wives' Club because we're not open to that type of change!

For fifteen years we've taken a couples trip every July. After a few years, the girls decided we could have fun (and more trips) without the men, so The Cube was formed. We take a girls' trip every January and keep a group text ongoing. We've been on beach trips, Broadway trips, lake vacays and spa trips.

We have supported one another as we began to lose our parents. We have shared joy in the marriages of our children, births of grandchildren, and shown love and sympathy through illness and loss. I am so grateful for this group of ladies who exemplify familial love and Southern kindness. It's a sisterhood. We even created a cookbook for our children.

One of the Cindy's (yes, there are three of us) shared this story about her mother growing up in Jackson, Mississippi: One day her mother and uncle, as children, took the bus to downtown Jackson. They were barefooted and made their way up to a pretty home and got in line at the gathering, "making themselves a plate." It turns out, they were at the Governor's Mansion. When asked later by her mama, she said, "They sure have nice dishes at the **govament's house**!"

I do not use the term "best friend" lightly. But I have been blessed with several unbelievable friends in my lifetime.
And they are all nicer and better people than me.

BECKY

I met Becky in the eighth grade, back when junior high was awkward, but at least cyber bullying wasn't a thing. We survived learning to drive, early morning dance practices, and our high school years as "good girls." As adults, she lived in St. Louis, so we got to see each other pretty often. She adored being a wife and mother and took wonderful care of her health. But when we were only 36 she found out she had ~~some freak~~ a brain tumor. She had the purest heart, and was so very kind. She battled, but died when we were 48. I ache for her everyday.

I think Bec was drawn to me because I'm so outgoing, and I think accepting. She was talented and loving and fierce in her own precious way. She fought. I love her kids like my own.

TEE

Tee and I both married and moved to our small town the same year. A town with one stoplight, a struggling country club, a water tower painted with the team mascot, and a lot of pride. We shared the years becoming mamas and making our homes together. How lucky we were to have found one another. One time we drank wine and tried to cut out plaid skirts to sew. That was definitely a "fail." Tee and her family later moved to Mississippi, and I look forward to seeing her, and time at the beach with her. She can make and do anything she sets her heart to do — from sewing, upholstering, decorating, and now she has learned to draw.

Tee is a joy to watch enjoying karaoke and has the unique ability to be adorable when she is drinking. She loves to entertain and can make any holiday fun. They do "minute to win it" games, play night golf with glow balls, and she loves to make up contests and games. She has a servant's heart. She is the most content when family and friends are gathered 'round. She is a wonderful cook and makes it look effortless. I personally love to have people do things for me. As you can see, it's a win-win situation for me. A couple of days with Tee is the best vacation I know. And you'll never see Tee without lipstick. She's a naturally elegant Southern lady.

TWILLA

I was about 30 when Twilla and I connected. I often laugh about how we somehow have way more confidence than we probably should, and we don't even know why. She was an elementary principal, raised three fabulous sons as a single mom, and worked in my gift shop on Saturdays for 20+ years.

What a lifesaver she was providing the time I needed with my kids. We are both over 60 and are "a little fluffy", but we both think we're pretty fabulous. Not better than others, just loving life. Nobody cracks us up like we do. Twilla won't eat at a restaurant buffet. She says it stands for <u>B</u>ig <u>U</u>gly <u>F</u>at <u>F</u>olks <u>E</u>atin' <u>T</u>ogether. You'll never see one again without thinking about that! And later, you'll see I listed several phrases her daddy used.

We have the worst sense of direction. Literally, none. We got lost in Dallas once, well, several times... and she was yelling, "the purple ball is not on the blue line" while looking at the GPS. All the years we went to market together (Dallas, Atlanta, NYC showrooms to order merchandise for my gift shop), it never failed that we'd leave a booth and start walking the wrong way. And if someone trying to give us directions mentions East or West, our eyes just glaze over.

We have our own language of words and phrases acquired during our friendship:

A "get drunk, throw down, bonfire" — a wild party

Living in Shacktivity — shacking up/living together

Curfew or Cleveland — cleavage

Mamaw Hooter — who we look like when our outfit looks like an old grandma

Embrace phrases, even incorrect ones that have had an impact on your life. I'm sure you can think of some of your own. Some of Taylor's were:

batwonner — a majorette/twirler

harpoonist — a musician who plays the harp

So, back to Twilla. We count our blessings daily, because we have successful and loving children, we are retired, and we love time with our grandkids. We have time to just watch movies, go to the lake house, and pick out special gifts for friends.

She likes to thank Daddy Don for buying us the lake house. We get to go more often than Don, because...well, farming and hunting.

And she reminds me daily to not f*** this up for us!

She's book smart, but admits she lacks common sense occasionally. She said I could tell you that one time she tried to change a tire and jacked up the wrong side of the car. Why? Because when she had previously watched a tire being changed, that was the side that was elevated. Why? Because the flat was on that side.

She told me once she was chasing her oldest son in a circle while giving him a whuppin', (holding his arm) until she tripped over his legs and fell. They still laugh about it.

And Twilla taught me this: If you know you're going to say yes when asked to do something, get credit for doing it graciously. For instance, if someone asks you a favor, don't bemoan all the things you need to be doing instead, before accepting.

She loves to shop after a holiday to catch the sales. I pretty much want to just move on, but I respect that she thinks it's fun to get a deal. One time she was at a Michael's store, and all the Halloween merchandise was marked down 90%. Now, I'm not kidding when I tell you she's good with numbers ("Did you just do that in your head?"), but figuring 90% off can be a little complicated. An elderly black fellow was watching her compute and said, "If it be 90% off, it be 10% on… and that's a whole lot easier to figure!"

My only regret is that we didn't save all of those holiday sweaters we bought in the 90s, so we can wear them as roommates at the Leisure Lodge.

ALESIA

Alesia is my friend who can do everything. She's highly creative, is patient with me, can repair anything, has a gift for reading instructions, and gets things done. We raised our children together and have served The Lord and our church together for 38+ years. I'll never repay her for all the projects I volunteered to do and then dragged her in to help.

DEBBIE

Debbie taught me about putting things in the vault. That is how she keeps secrets. I'm not a very good secret keeper. I mean to be… but then I just blurt things out. I'm quite sure I've lost friends because of this. Twilla and Alesia once said I need to go to blabbermouth rehab, which they call Blab-Rehab for short. Once they made me keep a Blab-Rehab sticker on my car for about six months as punishment. Creative Alesia made it.

God put Debbie in my life right after Becky passed away. She rides with me to see my mama in the nursing home, just to keep me company. We had a waiter once in Dallas who said to us, "What can I do to make your day more pleasant?" We just looked at each other and thought, "Well, isn't that awesome?" I occasionally remember to say that to Don!

ANNE

Anne has been my mentor and has always been there for me. She did a lot to ease me into Southernness. Her daughters were our first "kids" and now they love my grand-twins.

SHEILA

Sheila is Tee's "other" best friend. (Because Tee and fam moved to Mississippi 30 years ago.) Sheila is hilarious, and the three of us have the absolute best time together. Sheila and Tee are wonderful golfers, and I've never done more than hit the ball into the windmill. Friends don't have to have everything in common. She makes me laugh until I cry.

SHAN

Some friends you have most of your life, and that has been Shan. Our husbands grew up together, we all went to college together, and though they haven't lived near us for years, we know each other's truths, and our stories, and the love and support is there. When she walks into my house, it's as if I saw her just the day before.

Y'all, get you some friends who pray for you, not talk about you. That's all I can say.

Over the Top

I'm including this topic here because it's completely my opinion. You're getting to know me, so here goes:

80

The pressure. Oh, the pressure to impress. When I was a little girl the birthday party was about the *cake*. My mom made a chocolate cake with white drizzly icing, from scratch. I knew it was a special day. My birthday was about getting to have friends come over with gifts and to play, and when it was over they ran home. In fact, my younger brother and I were born on Valentine's Day, four years apart. As I recall, we only had a party every other year. Times were simpler, but I never felt neglected.

(Note: There are a lot of Valentine babies, because it is nine months after Mother's Day. I'm sure several of these mothers would have rather gotten jewelry!)

When my kids were little, it was about the *theme*. So, the cake matched the theme and we began paying to have one made. We found plates and napkins to match the theme, and we had treat bags for the guests. I remember long nights sitting on the living room floor making party treat bags.

Now, thanks to Pinterest, parents plan elaborate birthday parties. They are then posted to Facebook, the all-encompassing world of perfection. Everything is documented and impressive. Poor moms of today; having to attain that perfection. It's exhausting.

Now, if that's your thing I'm not condemning your dedication. But I know most mothers feel such pressure to impress.

And the expense. Lord help us.

When I was a teenager we had mock *try-outs for cheerleading*. We were dropped off at the school for our final practice and had one last night to perfect the routines. Years later, a mother got her foot in the door — so when my daughter was a cheerleader, the moms were present for mock try-outs. Ugh. You know they were talking about all the girls, and really, how unfair.

Natalie was a ballerina. Each year at recital her dad would have a *small bouquet* to hand her when she came out when it was over. It was so sweet, and not a production. Now, however, it is. I think dancers get bouquets so often they're not as special.

I've hosted several baby showers and parties for brides. All that is required is an appreciative couple and a fairly prompt thank you note. After all, I helped give the party out of love and respect for the couple and their parents.

At some point the honoree started bringing small *gifts for all the hostesses*. A candle, some dried homemade pasta, a bottle of wine — lots of pressure to be creative. The idea of a hostess gift was born. Once again, this didn't have to start. It's such a needless expense when all that is required is a sincere thank you.

I did, however, **drink the Kool-Aid**, and when my daughter got married I had personalized notecards, cocktail napkin sets, etc. to distribute in thanks to the hostesses.

The *marriage proposal* now has pressure to be a thing. When Don asked me to marry him he walked into my apartment, asked me, and was done. He had driven 4 hours, and I'm sure he just wanted to have the task completed. It was sweet.

Now, fellows hire photographers to surreptitiously follow them around so they can capture the moment. Bridal magazines have contests seeking unique proposals. Often all the parents are on standby to celebrate afterwards. (Which is nice.) Personally, I think men don't need that pressure. Just another example of how complicated things have gotten.

Did you know *Prom-vitation or Promposal* is a thing? Poor little 16-year-old guys have to prove their undying love for their girlfriends by doing something creative and unique to get a prom date. Are we really supposed to think that is important to a high school junior? **No, ma'am.** It's all about the show... and Facebook. If moms didn't get involved the guys could get back to the awkward way of possibly being turned down.

They've also started the *HOCO PRO*. Homecoming dance proposal. Yep.

Having a *Valentine's Day* birthday, my mom always bought me heart shaped doilies. I spent hours making hand-cut valentines using red construction paper, paste, and those ~~chalky~~ conversation hearts. The valentines that I received were perforated, separated, with the name hastily written on the back in pencil. They were dropped in paper bags we decorated. I loved Valentine's Day.

Enter parents. Now they spend money on custom tags and spend hours attaching them to whatever product coordinates with the theme. I'm not condemning this practice, but so many families cannot afford this. And it removes the child from the excitement of preparing for the holiday. Children are making custom valentine boxes. I saw some cute ones that looked like deer stands and Minnie Mouse. Actually, I think craft projects that parents and children do together are awesome. But somehow, I think it's as much about Facebook as anything. Just my opinion.

When a mother gives birth and the husband uses the occasion to give her diamond earrings that's his choice. But calling it a *Push Gift* makes it a "thing" and puts pressure on other couples or the husband. When I gave birth, I got a baby. When Natalie had twins, she got two. It is a moving experience for the husband to see what his wife experiences, but gift or no gift, love can be expressed in many ways.

Oh my. Sorority *rush coaches*? And why do they call it recruitment now? (And pledges are now called PNMs, potential new members.)

First day of school signs are a huge event now. I love to see them, but when we were raisin' our kids, just getting them to stand next to each other and smile was an accomplishment.

Some farm wife jokingly took a picture of her husband holding a "First Day of Harvest" sign. I just about wet my pants.

And the *schools* now have the 100th Day of School, and Donuts with Dad, and muffins with me-maw, and so much more, that the poor moms better have a good system of keeping track of all they're supposed to be prepared for.

And apparently, if you are Southern and plan a Disney World trip, if your child doesn't have 6 or 7 matching Disney-themed monogrammed outfits that they will NEVER WEAR AGAIN, did you even go to Disney? At least they will be easy to spot in Magic Kingdom if you can remember what is the day's color.

A speaker once said, at a conference I attended, "What was a luxury to our parents has become a necessity to us." One TV. One car. You get the picture. I kind of like that millennials are less impressed with things and more satisfied with experiences. But have you seen how many Christmas trees some people decorate? Or how many pumpkins people display in their yard? I swear, we only had one.

Here are examples of things that are JUST WRONG:

My friend, Susan, teaches college hospitality classes, so she is in the thick of things concerning the younger generation's interpretation of correct etiquette. (I must add that this goes back to a lack of **good raisin'** by their mothers.) One example she gave was of the *dorm shower*. Just two months after giving a graduation gift (always appropriate are monogrammed towels and a towel wrap) she was invited to a dorm shower. The child had actually registered for her bedding and other needs. Parents should purchase the dorm refrigerators and bedding. Or they can insist their child spend some of that graduation money they hopefully have written thank you notes for.

Another example Susan gave was a *stock-the-wedding-reception-bar shower*. Really? Scale back your plans and have an afternoon wedding with punch. But don't expect your guests to relish the idea of providing your liquor. That's as tacky as having a cash bar at your reception.

Susan asked me to please hurry up with this manuscript.

She also shared this ~~abhorrent~~ Facebook post from a bride referring to her shower.

Facebook Post: Callie's Bridal Shower

Good evening lovely ladies. If you would like to bring a gift (you don't have to), please keep reading. If you cannot attend, but would still like to get me a gift, just ask me for my address or you can give it to me the next time I see you!

84

Our registry is on amazon.com. Find registry
at the top and search XXXXXXX. Other gift
ideas would be anything personalized (glasses,
coasters, picture frames, cutting boards,
welcome signs, pillows, blankets, ring holder, etc.)
We will also need some things to use during the
wedding, but would like to keep as keepsakes
(serving utensils, cake topper, champagne flutes,
guest book, photo album, etc.) The keepsake
items are kind of specific, so just text me, and I
can send you a link of what we want exactly. I
also like jewelry, spa stuff, and candles.

Expectant mothers are now having professional photo
shoots. In an attempt to become more and more elaborate, I have
seen a few ~~bare~~ exposed bellies. "A Southern lady practices
modesty," is all I have to say about that.

I love #dormroomsofmississippi
It's way over-the-top decorating at Mississippi State University,
so, y'all know it's too much. I cannot imagine what they look like
by semester exams.

I have many more examples of faux pas. They are the
chocolate pie from The Help. I love my friends, and my intent is
not to hurt feelings, but I'm sure you can think of a few

Part Four
Southern Parlance

All Southerners are bilingual. We understand how the rest of the country talks, and then we have our own special way of sayin' things.

Bless Your Heart

Sincerity is a virtue familiar to every Southern girl. We openly compliment others' children, a friend's haircut or her outfit.

We also bless hearts. It is usually said when someone loses a loved one or suffers an illness. It means, "I'm sincerely sorry, you poor thing,"

It is also used to thank someone for going the extra mile.

But it is also used when someone has committed a faux pas. This passive-aggressive put-down is obvious by the tone of voice. This could be used to refer to the young lady at the horse races with a too-short dress, or the one with ombré hair and too much make up. Honey, in the South that just means she needs to tend to those roots. **Bless her heart.**

Bless it — similar to **Bless your heart**, in the not nice sense.

Words Southerners Mispronounce

Library	Some tend to omit that first r.
Suite	The Nutcracker Suite. A bedroom suite. Not suit. That's what a man wears.
Voilà	People, it's not wallah.
Bob wire	Barbed wire.
Help	Some southerners use the word hope as in, "the treatment really hoped me a lot."
"For Sell"	... sometimes used for For Sale.
Ideal	Idea. "What a great ideal!"
Get a holt of	Get ahold of, locate

Hisself   "He cut hisself."

As for grammar, I wish people understood they are not "apart" of a group, but "a part."

And I like the term, "grammar police" as I DID teach junior high English for a couple of years. Teaching English was easy for me, because my parents had good grammar. I loved diagramming sentences, so call me a nerd if you'd like.
It was a struggle undoing the way some children had been taught at home.

I majored in French at university and it was a breeze to learn because of my English background. The whole loving other cultures thing worked to my advantage, too.

With Facebook, people began to express their opinions, and without knowing it, their grammatical errors were exposed. If adults don't know their, there and they're, your and you're, a lot vs. alot, that it's specific and not Pacific, to and too, they just can't hide their ignorance.

Many people say, "That's just who I am. I don't care." But I would hope that trying to improve oneself would be a continuous attempt.

In fact, Southern want ads and Facebook sale pages can be very entertaining. Looking for a *slay bed* or *a chester draws*? How 'bout some *parma jawn* cheese for your pizza?

Words Southerners Mispronounce and it's Perfectly Okay

Nekked   Naked.
Bar pits   Borrow pits are the ponds that run along the Mississippi River levee, thus called because they were created when holes were dug, and dirt was borrowed, to build the levee.
Stomp   Stamp your foot, stomp on a bug.
              Also refers to a dance hall.
Vi-doc   Railroad viaduct

Words and Phrases Southerners Use That Yankees Don't Get

Y'all

It's not gender specific (How do y'all say "you guys" to a bunch of girls?) and it falls off the tongue easily. It even means large groups, as in "Are all y'all going to the movie?"

Y'all vs. you guys:

My grand twins live in Northwest Arkansas. At their daycare they learned to say, "Come on you guys." It **tickles me** as well as leaves me mortified.

Y'all 'd've — y'all would have. As in, " Y'all 'd've loved the rodeo last weekend."

Things we say upon greeting:

Hey   This is how we say "Hi!"

Hey, y'all!   … is the true Southern greeting.

How y'all dooooin'?

Let me hug your neck.

How's ur momma 'n 'em?

I haven't seen you in a coon's age.

Gimme some sugar   … means a kiss. Don't go after some sugar in the kitchen.

Whatcha know good?

As I live and breathe!

You're a sight for sore eyes   I haven't seen you in so long, what a pleasure!

Who are your people? Southerners like to feel connected to people we meet.

Pleasure ta meet ya!

Well, I'll be!

"Knock knock" What we holler when we walk in someone's door.

Look what the cat dragged in!

Terms about health:

He's **down in his back.**

Puny In the north it means small. In the South is means sickly.

Stove up ... means you can barely move you're so sore, achy, or constipated.

Spell ... feeling light headed or faint — As in, "She had one of her spells after shooing that bird out of the kitchen."

Tarred, **TI-rd** (depending on where you live in the South) tired.

My dogs are barking My feet are killing me

Girl, he was sick as a dawg. Throwing up

Plum tuckered out

She's got one foot in the grave.

Down with Has an ailment, as in, "Miss Hattie's down with the rheumatism today."

I'm give out So tired I can barely move

Doctor that cut   ... as in, take care of it.

Worn slap out   How I feel after working all day in my yard.

"Mr. Billy done woke up dead."   He died in his sleep.

Eat up   "She's eat up with cancer" or "The baby's eat up with a rash."

Miss Katherine's not long for this world.   Close to death

She's got a sick headache. Migraine.

I'm feelin' poorly today.   Not well

Runnin' a tempachur   Has a fever

Impropriety

Everything she's got is out on the showroom floor — said when talking about a woman with a bad reputation.
        Also,
 I have heels higher than her standards.
        And,
Her skirt's so short you can see to Christmas!

Actin' the ho — inappropriate behavior

She's kinda skanky

Easy pickin's — refers to a girl who is drunk and may be easy.

Sweatin' like a whore in church.

<u>Them's fightin' words</u>

Bitch slapped

Cold cocked

She was on him like a duck on a June bug.

Whup ass   Beat up or whip, or you can open a can of it

Come to fisticuffs

I'm gonna **snatch you bald headed**

He's **bowed up**   Ready to fight, of ill humor, really built up from weight lifting

I'll cut you four ways: long, deep, wide and repeatedly.

Slap or knock **upside the head**

Ruckus   Disturbance, fight or commotion

She **slapped the mess outta** him.

Get crossways with someone   Have a disagreement

<u>Phrases we get from farmin':</u>

Fair to middlin'   An answer to "How are you doing?" Meaning fairly well. Good Middling is the USDA's term for the best grade of cotton.

He worked 'til **dark thirty.**   Half hour past sunset

They worked **from can to can't**. Referred to someone picking cotton from the time he could see daybreak to the evening when they could no longer see.

We're **in the short rows** now. In farmer talk it means the job is nearly finished.

Livin' (or walkin') in high cotton Feeling wealthy or particularly successful

He's **in the back 40** (acres)

Livin' **high on the hog**

White gold — cotton

Lost my cotton pickin' mind

Just a cotton pickin' minute

Laid by — when all crops are in the ground. Watering is done, and just waiting on harvest.

Phrases with critters:

I don't have a dog in that fight/I ain't got a dog in that hunt I don't have an opinion one way or another

He's so lazy he wouldn't **hit a lick at a snake**.

Puttin' on the dog Fancy, or going all out

Bird dogs set birds That's just the way it is

Let me tell ya **how the cow ate the cabbage** Let me tell you how it is.

Ya lie down with dogs, ya get up with fleas.

Watch out for deer!   That's Southern for "I love you!" Or be careful.

Pill Bugs are called **Rollie-Pollies**

If it had been a snake it woulda bit ya.

Let sleepin' dogs lie.

Fish or cut bait   Telling someone to get the job done

I double dog dare you

Nekked as a jaybird

That dog'll hunt   We can do that

Lightenin' bugs   Fireflies

Full as a tick

I don't give a rat's ass

Like water off a duck's back   It doesn't sink in

Varmint   Wild animal

Worthless as tits on a boar hog

Gotta do some rat killin'   Get some chores done

She doesn't have **sense God gave a goose**

Our Southern descriptions of folks:

Precious   Can be sincere, or not.

Full o' piss and vinegar

Tow-headed   A blond child

Doofus   Dork, bumbler

She's all **high-falootin'** now.   To think highly of oneself, pretentious

Taller than a Georgia pine

He's tough as a pine knot

She's knee high to a grasshopper

He's older 'n dirt

Ornery   Pronounced awwn-ree —troublemaker, combative, bad tempered, troublesome child, or old person.

Mess   ... as in, "looking a fright", but doesn't always mean unkept.   She's somethin' else, as in "**a hot mess**"

Mean as a snake

Tight wad   Stingy, an old skinflint, cheap as dirt

She was limp as a dishrag

She **favors** you   Similar in looks

So stinkin' cute or **Cute as a bug**

Dirt poor

You ain't right   Said joking with a friend who says or does something questionable or inappropriate

He ain't right   Could refer to someone's lack of a high IQ

He ain't no fool

She's blind in one eye and can't see out of the other   She doesn't have a clue

She's a force to be reckoned with.

He was the **turd in the punchbowl**   A nuisance or problem who ruined everything

He's **sorry as hell**

Pretty as a peach

He ain't got a **lick 'a sense.**

Butter wouldn't melt in her mouth

Rode hard and put up wet   Refers to a horse, but in this context, it's used to describe a woman who's had a rough day

She's wound up tighter than a girdle on a fat Baptist preacher's wife at an all-you-can-eat pancake breakfast.

She got **too big for her britches**   Her newfound wealth has gone to her head.

They look like **country come to town**

Uppity   Snobbish or arrogant

He's the **spittin' image** of his daddy.

She's not **big as a minute**

Crazy heifer Wild, crazy, often obese, woman

He's plumb crazy Completely out of his mind

Locations and distance:

Over yonder or **up yonder** a little way off

A right far piece Farther than yonder

Brick A long time or far away. In Virginia, as in, "I haven't seen you in a brick."

Catty-corner, kitty-corner Diagonally across the street.

Down the street Close by

Up 'n 'ere Yes, Sheila, I've got to tell them about when we were in Ephesus, Turkey, outside the Library of Celsus and you said, "Y'all wanna go up 'n 'ere?"

Smack dab "He left his underwear smack dab in the middle of the floor."

He's from off Moved here, but not from the South

You're not from around here, are ya?

Up under Did you check up under the bed?

Hemmed in As in "We hemmed in the snake and then he caught it."

Stompin' grounds Familiar surroundings, hometown. As in, "It's sure is good to be back in my ol' stompin' grounds."

Fronchard   As opposed to the backyard.

Where y'at?

The Coronavirus in the South

I was about to publish when I stayed most of three months at the house. It wasn't easy for anyone. I was luckier than most, living in a sparsely populated area. For Southerners, social distancing goes against who we are! 2020 was the waste of a good Erin Condren Daily Planner, and the best my yard has looked in years. Every preacher became a televangelist, too. Facebook even invented the new "care" emoji, that to us means, "Bless your heart."

We referred to the unfortunate time as "The Covid." Facebook's *Cooking with Brenda Gantt* kept me sane, and @thelesliejordan made me laugh every day.

Stay yo' ass at home. What people should've done during the Coronapocalypse. (And parents will remember it as the longest Spring Break ever.)

...or as some said, the **Corn Virus.**

Corn-teen   Quarantine

Hunker down   How Southerners "Shelter in place."

If you've ever stepped on a sweetgum ball, picked it up, and looked at it, it looks just like the picture of the Coronavirus. There's nothin' sweet about those spiky devils.

Not enough headings for the rest of these:

We call our grocery carts **buggies**

We **mash** the button on an elevator or push it. We don't say press.

We say **fixin' to** (or **fitinta**) when we're about to do something.

Fixin's are the lettuce and tomato on a burger, fries on the side, or slaw on your barbecue sandwich.

Carry   I hope the Hogs carry (win) the game! (Arkansas Razorbacks! **Wooooo Pig Sooie!**)

Carry   Having a handgun on your person.

Bit   A little bit, not referring to part of the bridle.

Clicker, flipper, moken troll   TV remote

Recliner chair.   Redundant, I know.

Honey   Can be a dire warning or a term of endearment. Learn to discern.

Wraslin'   Wrestling with a conflict or problem

Cher   Endearing or cute. From the French. Used in Louisiana, thus Cajun French. Commonly they say, **Cher Bébé**, which means, "What a cute baby!"

Tater	potato
Mater	tomato
Gator	alligator
Far	fire
Minner	minnow
Nanner	banana
Skeeter	mosquito
Borry	borrow
Tar	tire
Winda	window
Pilla	pillow
Jury	jewelry
Pitcher	photo ... As in, "**pitcher day** at school!"

Holler	Hollow, as in a narrow valley found in the Appalachians
Holler	Letting someone know, as in, "Holler if you need anything!"
Commode	The potty or toilet
Warshrag	Washcloth
Laundromat	Washateria
Doohicky	Thingamabob, thingamajig, whatchamacallit
Putt Putt	Miniature golf
Service Road	Access road
Tump	Knock over a glass of milk or flip over in a canoe (Yes, it's a combo of tip and dump.)
Tote	To carry "Please help me tote in these groceries." In some parts of he South, a tote is a bag.
Bag	What they put your groceries in. Not a sack.
Fiddlefart or **lallygag**	To dawdle or spend time aimlessly
The law	Not just "the regulations," but the police. As in, "I called **the law** on his **sorry ass**."
Sop	Using a rag to clean up a spill, or a piece or bread in your gravy.
Ear bobs	What everyone's grandmother called earrings. She also called blush **rouge** and a handbag a **pocketbook**.

Play purdies Toys. As in, Grandma said, "Her play purdies are **strown** all over this house."

Fireboard   What older folks call the fireplace mantel

Ice Box   What older folks call the refrigerator

Ten full   Aluminum foil.

Gettin' some color Getting a tan or putting on make up.

A **color**   A crayon

Flat   Simply   **She flat out lied.**
                       He flat killed her dead.

Cut   Turn something off. As in, "Cut off the fan when you leave." If the electric company **cuts off your lights** it means you've been disconnected; and, to stab someone, or to open or remove something with a sharp object

Y'all be careful Doesn't mean you're threatened. It's just a way to tell someone goodbye and to have a safe trip.

Make my picture! When we want you to take our photo.

Reckon? You think or guess, as in, "Reckon they're awake?"

Might coulda/might shoulda

You **might oughta**...

Jeet yet? Did ya eat yet?

Tea Leaf? Did he leave?

Monebac   Said when directing someone backing up a pick up or inviting your guests to return soon (Come on back)

Yawnto   Do you want to? "Yawnto come by later and watch the race?"

Rat cheer   Right here

Now, whatchasayin'?   Sorry, I don't understand.

'Mon now   C'mon, let's go

Pra-luh-so   Probably so

A'ight Now   Hello. Goodbye. You better watch out 'cause I've about had enough of that.

Don't that just take the cake!   What a surprise!

I tell you what   An exclamation. As in, "I tell you what, she really knows how to season some greens."

Dadgum, dagumm, or **dadburn**   "I spilled my dagumm nail polish on my bedspread."

Dadgummit, dagnabit   Said at the beginning of a statement when you are frustrated.

Wappy-jawed or **wampy-jawed**   Askew

Frou Frou   With lace and ruffles, or curlicued lettering

I've never.... in all my days

Spell   A measure of time — As in, "Come sit a spell up on the porch with me."
      — Or, forming words by putting letters together
      — 'bout to faint
      — giving someone a break — **"I'll spell you."**

Pick up   The most common mode of Southern transportation

— Also, to collect a pizza from the pizza place
— Or, to move something from a low to high place
— When you hook up with someone in a bar

What a **humdinger**   Remarkable or outstanding

Scared the livin' daylights outta me

Got a mind to   Thinking about doing something

Do what?   Are you kiddin' or serious?

Do what now?   In the north, they say, "huh?'

What?   What a Southern girl says when she wants to give her boyfriend a chance to change his story,

Jus' sayin'!   "That bow was too big for that baby. Jus' sayin'."

Mess   Also refers to a unit of measure: mess of greens or mess of fish

Messin'   Fooling around. "We were just messin' around." (Said by kids caught doing something they shouldn't be doin')
       Also, being unfaithful. "I heard Joseph's been messin' around with that new girl."

Put (or pull) the door to   Shut the door

Swoll   As in the creek, or your knee, or from a bug bite

Titty Bar   Gentlemen's Club or Strip Club

Caddywampus or **caddawompas** means askew or unconventional. We use all of these words.

Hit   Refers to striking someone, unless you're following directions — "Take this road till it hits Highway 4."

Somethin' awful As is, "I miss her somethin' awful."

Ah mo I'm going to, as in "Ah mo go on now and get the yard mowed."

I yoosta could cut a stack a wood in a couple of hours.

Britches Trousers

Too big for her britches A child who probably needs a spankin'.

Draws Underpants or drawers

Hot dang!

Are they blood kin?

Keep talkin'! You better be quiet and change your attitude

Sho-nuff Sure enough

Goodness gracious! Lawd hammercy! Oh, my goodness! Lord have mercy!

You're barkin' up the wrong tree.

You're preachin' to the choir. I completely agree

Drekley Directly, which means soon; in a few minutes

Ganked up or **ganky** As in someone's teeth

Pallet A bed made with blankets on the floor. It's not sleeping on a pallet made of wood. Whenever we had thunderstorms our kids slept on a pallet at the foot of our bed.

Packing As in packin' heat (a gun)

Mushmelon   A cantaloupe

Love me some   As in, "Love me some George Strait!" Or "Love me some tater salad."

Likes   Lacks, as in, "He likes 300 acres of pickin' (cotton)."

Land sakes

Tarnation   Replaces the word Hell, as in, "What in tarnation have you done?"

Hallelujah, and pass the collection plate   I totally agree, it's about time

Fiddlesticks

Boy, howdy

Good gravy!   Oh my gosh.

Likely   As in more than likely

Showin' out   Showing off. But also used, "Mary Lou's roses are really showin' out!"

Yee Haw!

Ax to grind

On accident   A mistake, unintended mishap. "I deleted the football game he had dvr'ed on accident."

I'm **proud for ya**   As in, "Your grandchild is beautiful. I'm proud for ya."

Proud   She knows she looks good.

— Also, if you are proud of something, you are asking too much money for it. **She's proud of that.**

God love it, God love her

By and by   Eventually

Pert near   Pretty near/close

Hammy downs   Hand me downs. Older sibling's clothes

Water fountain   Drinking fountain

Yard sale   Garage sale, rummage sale or tag sale

Trash can   Garbage can

Gaumed up   Messed up, as in, the floor.

Eighteen-wheeler   Semi-truck or tractor trailer

Tennis shoes, or **tenny shoes**   We don't call 'em sneakers like they do "way up North."

Diddly squat   Nothin', zero. "She didn't even help clear the table. She didn't do diddly squat."

It was a **rough as a corncob**

Short end of the stick   Getting treated unfairly

That **beats all** I've ever seen

Everwhichaway   "Those bees busted outta that hive going everwhichaway."

Nary   None

Hurry up! We're burning daylight. Wastin' precious time.

Come hell or high water
Turnabout is fair play

... as all get out   As in, **She's mean as all get out.**

Spittin' nails Very angry

Give her the what for Let her know what you really think

Oh, my lands! Oh, my stars!

Humdinger An outstanding or remarkable person, place or thing

Have you lost your ever-lovin' mind? Said when someone does something they shouldn't have

Get it while the gettin's good.

Shut yo' mouth Hush or be quiet with that foolishness

She's about to run me ragged.

Back in the day... we had to get up to change the channel.

All tore up   — can refer to a truck engine
                    — or a drunk girl
                    — reaction to bad news

Nasty To Yankees it means dirty. To Southerners it refers to distasteful food.

Ugly/ Quit bein' ugly Means stop being mean or actin' out.

In a tizzy Frazzled, nervous energy, got your **panties in a wad.**

Hand to God Used when we are really serious in what we're saying. Used instead of, "I swear to God."

Get to gettin' Used in Georgia, meaning it's time to leave or go

Quit yer belly achin' Stop whining

Kindly Kind of. As in, "She's kindly nice."
     Also, **Thank ya kindly.**

Darlin' I had the sweetest older friend, and I can still hear her voice in my head sayin' "darlin.'"

Package store Where Mississippians go to buy their liquor

Air-up Inflate, as in a pool float or tires

Get tickled Amused, makes one laugh

Pee your pants Wet oneself

Whuppin' Spanking

I tell you what... Yes, folks, that is a complete sentence. As in, "Have you seen how pretty that oldest Martin daughter is?" "I tell you what."

Fit to be tied

I 'bout fell out Shocked to see or hear something

That's a bald faced lie! (or, bold faced)

Who are your people? Southerners like to feel connected to people we meet.

It'll all come out in the wash It will work out.

He's got a right smart way of doin' things.

Fool   Southerners love this word. If you are from the South, jot down a few ways you've used this word:

Damn fool   The damn fool drove off in the ditch.

Fool-headed

Act a fool   As in, "You should've seen her at her ex's funeral. Lord, she acted a fool."

Disgraceful and **Pitiful** are words we love to use, too.

Fine is another great Southern word.

So is **ignernt**   Ignorant, as in **"That was a durn ignernt thing to do!"**

Mighty or **Right**   Extra, as in, **"She's right talented."**

Mighty fine

Slap   Totally, completely

He's a sorry excuse for a human being.

He needs to simmer down.
Martha's **got some dirt** on that Thompson girl. (gossip)

I've never seen **the likes of such.** (anything like it)

Clean the yard   Get rid of everything

Cukaburs   The dog's ears were covered in **cukaburs.** (cockleburs.)

Pulley bone   Wish bone, breast piece of fried chicken

Carpetbaggers   Yankee who came to Dixie for profit and not good intentions

Y'all ain't right   This is a response given to a friend who has said something a little out of character, or unkind, or ridiculous. As in, you aren't of sound mind.

Hunky Dory   Just fine

Supper   The evening meal. We have Sunday dinner at lunchtime. Even though a dinner party is at night, we know it's supper. Yes, it's complicated.

I don't care to   In Eastern Tennessee when asked to do something, the response, **"I don't care to"** means I don't mind doing it, no worries.

Showed his butt   Misbehaved

Givin' someone grief   Ribbing someone, giving them a hard time.

Drekkly   In the north they may go directly to the Principal's office, but it the South it refers to pretty soon… "I'll be there directly."

Don't get me started…

She'll **line you out… in a heartbeat.**

I mona gitchy   "I'm gonna get ya!" Said when tickling a child.

Used to could   Was able to do something before getting old or had an accident

Nary a piece   She didn't save nary a piece of pie for her husband.

Ankle biter Baby

skeedaddle or skedaddle Leave, or go away quickly

Ruint or **Rurnt** Messed up or destroyed; ruined. **She done ruint that dog, lettin' her sleep on the bed.**

Wreck Can be an auto accident, but often means something looks bad, "Her room is a wreck," or "My hair looks a wreck."

Striped We sometimes pronounce, **stripe-ed**. "She wore those hideous **stripe-ed** leggin's and that **Pokey-Dotted** top.

Somethin' awful Terribly bad, as in diaper rash.

Drounded Drowned. "Bless them. She done drounded in the river."

You're so cute I could **eat you with a spoon!**

He did her wrong/ She did him wrong Unfaithful

Puttin' up peas or **put up the iron** doesn't refer to the direction UP. It means put away or prepared.

The milk turned It is sour, out of date.

"Gimme some sugar!" Means a kiss. Don't go after some sugar in the kitchen.

Laying out Can refer to getting a tan, skipping class, or missing work
She could **charm the dew off the honeysuckle**

In front of God 'n everybody as in, "When she fell off the dance floor, her dress flew up in front of God 'n everybody."

Ugly as homemade sin/soap

Gee haw   Usually used as, "We just don't gee haw." Meaning, try as you might, you just don't seem to connect with that person. But it doesn't mean you dislike them.

Don't be ugly   Does not refer to one's physical appearance, but refers to behavior.

Tookie   Refers to a misbehavin' child

That lie fell off her tongue slick as butta.

Much obliged   Most appreciated

Meddlin'   Interfered or bothering

Like white on rice   Not a racial slur — sticking together

Awallago, or **wall ago**   A while ago

Narry a thing   Nothing

He's **"good people"**

She's got **home trainin'**

Lawd, help!   Or, Lord, help us!

Lawsy   Oh, Lord!

Dang sure

Take your sweet time.

Got a mind to...   Thinking about doing something

You **mightotta** (might ought to) A polite way of suggesting someone should do something

If the Good Lawd's willin' and the creek don't rise.

She was actin' out this afternoon and likely needed a spankin'.

Who made the tea? This tea is nasty.

How 'bout them Hogs? As Arkansas Razorback fans, this is what someone throws out to stop a conversation and change the subject.

As all get out To the max

We resemble As in, my granddaughter and I look alike.

"Don't **give me grief** about supper not bein' ready."

Fly Flop, Fly Flott, Floss water Fly swatter

I tell you what... (insert story here) **... Ain't that the truth?**

Messin' and gommin' Not accomplishing much. Also, **Lollygag Piddle fart,** and **Fiddle fart.**

Call ya out Catch someone in a lie, or dare them to fight.

Why, he ain't no count Worthless

"**I 'bout died ...** when I saw Sue Ellen's hair!"

I like to never...

The more you stir it, the more it stinks.

Feels like **a month of Sundays** Due to **"Blue Laws"** where alcohol is not sold, this refers to a long day with no amusement.

Mondee, Tuesdee, Wensdee   You get it

Butter my biscuits!   I'll be darned!

Do what now?   What are you saying?

Beg pardon   I beg your pardon

I'm **serious as a heart attack.**

Matchy-matchy   As in dressing your children alike.

She **chewed him up and spit him out.**   Gave him **a good cussin'**

Now we're **cookin' with gas**   Making progress

Have a hankerin' for   As in, "My precious mother in law gets a hankerin' for a Frosty from Wendy's"

"Hurry y'all. We've gotta beat the Baptists to the buffet."

Fit to be tied

U-sta   As in, I **u-sta** be able to do more before I **got down in my back**.

I'm hanging out like a **hair in a biscuit**   Out of place

Scat   Said when someone sneezes,
or when shooing a cat away

Shut the front door!   An expression of surprise
That's some **good groceries!**   Compliments a delicious meal

Making groceries   Going shopping

We need to have a "come to Jesus" meeting. Usually heard as your mother is dragging you away by your ear.

Flatter than a fritter

Sober as a judge

Good God Almighty! Y'all need Jesus!

Wolfin' or scarfin' down food

Don't bite off more 'n you can chew.

Quit your bellyachin'.

Thump   As in, "I'm gonna thump you upside the head!"

Going to Egypt, hit the bushes; see a man about a horse
        To the privy

Gussied up All dressed up

It don't make me no never-mind. I don't care one way or the other.

I haven't seen **hide nor hair** of your brother.

You good?   Can mean... No need to say sorry
                        Do you want some more?
                        Need money?
                        Are you okay?
                        You can stop talking.

Mightotta A polite way of saying you should. "You mightotta wear khakis to the party."

Sunday week   A week from Sunday

Honkin'   As in, "We ordered a big ol' honkin' steak!"

High waters   Trousers that are too short

Woods   In the south we don't call it the forest.

...as all get out   As in, "She's ugly as all get out!"

I ain't playin'   Not kidding

I'm just sayin'

Shag   Dancing in the Carolinas. Not the same as shagging in the UK.

Jacked up   Excited or high

I like to (have) hurt myself... As in, ate too much, or running from a snake

She comes from ol' money.   Inherited riches

Chill Bumps   Goose bumps

Give 'em the stink eye

It's the devil   Referring to something you can't keep away from... like Aunt Sue's Italian cream cake.

He's about to run me crazy

Juice   Electricity

Up   A little word we add when talkin' about cleanin'. Tidy up, straighten up and clean up

Cur-us   Not curious as in inquisitive, but as in peculiar. "He don't like ham-beans, he's kinda cur-us."

High tailin' it Gettin' after it, moving quickly away

Bust a gut Laughing so hard

Watcha need? What can I do/get for you?

On the regular Hey go to the boat (casino) on the regular.

Ima I'm about to …

Burnt me up Made me mad

Big'un "Went fishin' today and caught me a big'un.

Flat out lied

In a New York minute — quickly

Give me grief Tease, give a hard time

I didn't know him from Adam.

Bud vase A small floral arrangement. **"I sent a bud vase when she got on the Homecoming Court."**

Blew up her phone Called and called

I'd rather **take a bullet** than go to your mama's for Christmas.

Tote To carry

Pitiful A sickly child can be pitiful. An apple pie can be pitiful. A vegetable garden can be pitiful.

Skeez A guy who will try to kiss another man's wife on the mouth. A narcissistic guy who probably screws around.

Dunn for money Ask someone who has borrowed from you, or owes your place of business, to pay up

Shindig A gathering or party

Sweatin' like a sinner on Sunday

He's tryin' my patience! Getting on my nerves

C'mere Come here

Wallerin' When your kids constantly climb all over you
                —Or, consumed with, "Wallerin' in sorrow."

Y'all qweeeit Quit, stop.

That beats all

She's spinninanight We are having a sleepover.

He's happier than a tornado in a trailer park.

"The bigger the hair, the closer to God."
                                        — Dolly Parton.

The bigger the bow, the better the Mom.

Butt naked When someone goes skinny dippin' or strips down.

Buck wild Refers to a teenager that cannot be controlled, or a girl who goes crazy when she goes off to college.

Stop stirring the soup Causing trouble

Not having a pot to piss in Urine was once used to tan animal hides. Only "piss poor" people depended on this practice of selling to the tannery. Not being able to afford a pot was the poorest of the poor.

<u>Don't let your memaw read these:</u>

Shit outta luck

Bored shitless

Som Bitch Son of a bitch — as in, "The sombitch slit my tires!"

Ugly summmmbitch S.O.B

He done shit and fell back in it. He really messed up.

She done shit in her nest.

I'll tell you one thing, (always followed by) **you sorry S.O.B.**

Dayum Yes, two syllables.

Sorry, my ass. Means you know they're not really sorry.

Are y'all shittin' me? My son-in-law's response when my daughter informed him they were expecting twins!

They done lost their damn mind.

Shit or get off the pot. Make up your mind

Busier than a one-legged man in an ass kickin' contest.

Can't **make this shit up**

Shit fire and save the matches.

Hot damn!

A shit ton A whole lot. My grand twins say, "A boat yoad." (They have trouble with Ls.)

Sorry ass   As in, "He can walk his own sorry ass home."

Sorry, my ass   I don't believe you're sorry.

Haul ass   As in, home, after curfew.

The bigger the O (hoop earrings), **the bigger the (w)HO(re).**

He done banged her like a screen door in a hurricane.

Why the Hell not?

The hell you say.

Showing your butt (or ass) doesn't mean you pulled your pants down. It means you were misbehaving.

Maddernhell   Really upset.

Half-assed   Don't do a half-assed job of rakin' the yard.

Some of Twilla's daddy's best phrases:
  "Ode to Mr. Thad"

No tell motel   Where a couple meets for a rendez-vous

We're going all around by Laura's house   Taking the long way, possibly lost

He wants her bulldog/She wants his bulldog   Refers to attraction to another
Ya dance with the one that brung ya.

She fell from the top branch of the ugly tree.

That face looks like it wore out two bodies.

Junin' around   Doing a lot of nothing around the house

Southern Sports Sayings:

Ridin' the pine

Tailgating   Hanging out before a football game; eating and drinking with friends. Participants wear team colors and enjoy talkin' trash about the opponent. See also, riding another car's tail when driving.

Whatcha got on the game?

Beat ya by a nose.

He's bowed up like a Banty rooster

Armchair quarterback

He jumped the gun
The whole nine yards

He's got some skin in the game

Rippin' lips (refers to fishing)
What you'll hear at a Southern gathering

"C'mon y'all", someone calls from another room, **"It's time to say the blessing!"**

Hung over phrases:

I'm so sick I'd have to get better to die.

I feel like a bagga smashed assholes.

I feel like I got eaten by a bear and shit off a cliff.

When kids are young, they play the "Yo' mamma" game, teasing each other. As adults, there are a couple of phrases about homeliness that I love:

I wonder what she would charge to haunt a house?

His momma borrows another baby for church.

<u>Terms for crazy:</u>

She's certified crazy

Crazy as a Betsy bug

Bat shit crazy

Nuttier than a squirrel turd

About a bubble off plumb   Referring to a carpenter's level

She's three gallons of crazy in a two-gallon bucket

The cheese done slid off of his cracker

It's been said that we (Southerners) don't hide crazy. We just put her out on the front porch for everyone to see.

<u>I love dimwitted phrases:</u>

His cornbread ain't done in the middle.

She's not the sharpest knife in the drawer/tool in the shed. He's one brick shy of a load.

The porch light's on, but no one's home.

He's a few cards short of a deck.

He's only got one oar in the water.

She's a few fries short of a Happy Meal.

He's so dumb, he could throw himself on the ground and miss.

His elevator doesn't go all the way to the top.

<u>Some things Don's friend Chuck said that made me laugh:</u>

I'd marry her brother just to get in the family.

It'll all make a turd. (Whether eating a fine meal or a Big Mac)

<u>Lord, have mercy!</u>

This one reminds me of a cute story.

My first housekeeper was a kind woman named Mercy. She ironed and dusted and visited with my children. One Sunday in Church we did a responsive prayer with "Lord, have mercy upon us." Taylor, who was about four, looked at me and said quite loudly, "Why are y'all talking about Mercy?"

Wanna hear some other cute kids' stories?

Once, Nan was leading children's church and asked the kids if they ever did anything to help their parents. One little girl piped up and said, "Sometimes I watch my baby sister while Momma and Daddy take a shower together." Years later we found out the "younger sister" was one of Natalie's college roommates.

Taylor also said, "God can do everything, but I can make the doors open at Piggly Wiggly."

We convinced Taylor that if he went to jail, all they would feed him was bread and water. One day in the grocery store we saw a police officer. He turned to me and said, "He must be here to buy the bread, because water is free." (This was before bottled water hit the U.S.)

Tee's son, Will, was rubbing her unshaved legs one day when he was young, and said, "Momma, you have a million splinters!"

"It was un-ble-bla," is now a family saying. Will wrote a journal in the first grade. Tee called me crying/laughing at the end of the year when he brought it home. Whatever he had been describing, he said was "unbelievable".

Southern Superstitions and Unique Sayin's

Once a black cat crossed the road in front of Twilla and me. That meant we immediately had to make the block. Unfortunately, I went down a one-way street and we were stopped by a cop. Luckily, the police officer understood, when we explained what had happened!

Granny (my mother-in-law) says, when you give a wallet or billfold as a gift always put money IN it.

Or you're cutting your luck

Open the window, following a death, to let the soul out.

Never give a pocketknife as a gift, as it'll cut your friendship.

If your palm is itching, you'll come into some money.

Hold your breath in a tunnel. Lift your feet when driving over RR tracks.

Spit in one hand, wish in another. See which one fills up the fastest.

If a frog had wings he wouldn't bump his butt every time he hopped.

Don't do housework on New Year's Day. You'll sweep out the good luck.

Leave from the same door you entered.

Whistling past a graveyard and throwing salt over your shoulder are both done to ward off bad luck.

Southern Colorful Characters

I once knew a shorter fellow. His nickname from high school was "tittie high." You get the picture.

In our town, there was a man who was known to have driven a school bus in reverse from Pine Bluff (about an hour away). His nickname became Bus Driver, or Bus for short. His real name was Delbert Odom. That's a good Southern name.

Stump / Hammerhead / T Bone / Peanut / Booger / Punkin' / Biggun / Jimbo / Sonny are just a few examples.

Southern women are often given nicknames. My college roommate's name is Teensy. I've known ladies called Kissy, Tootie, and Tootsie.

Every Southern family has a Bubba and a Sissy.

I heard about a family who had twin boys. They named the firstborn "Charles, Jr." and the other "Charles, III" and they call them Junior and Trey.

Part Five
Rules about Actin' Right

Raisin' the Little Ones

How many years ago do you think Fred Astaire said this? "The hardest task kids face today is learning good manners without seeing any." It is our job to teach our children to be kind and considerate human beings.

Train up a child in the way he should go: and when he is old, he will not depart from it.
— Proverbs 22:6

Children, marriages, and flower gardens reflect the kind of care they get.
— Unknown

If you raise your children, you can spoil your grandchildren. If you spoil your children, you'll have to raise your grandchildren.
— Unknown

My Mom and Dad's parenting style was teamwork. I never wanted my parents to be disappointed in me. Shame was the worst punishment. Don thinks I needed more spankin's.

A Southern mother knows there is nothing worse than sassiness. It just cannot be tolerated. Everyone knows a sassy child will become a heathen, and eventually end up in the penitentiary. That's the progression.

What Southern parents strive for:
Hearing, **"Her mama raised her right."**
And we love being told, **"She favors you!"**

So, parents:
Teach gratitude. Teach kindness.

Show respect to everyone and your children will learn that from you.

Use the phrases, "Mind your manners." and "Use your inside voice."

"Mind your manners" means do not ask for food at someone's house, do not go through their drawers, and always say "please" and "thank you." It also means, don't whine when we leave, and please hug everybody.

Ask them, "What's the magic word?" if they don't say "please."

Or, "What do you say?" And the answer is, "thank you."

Your children are NOT invited to a party or wedding if they are not specifically listed on the envelope. Your children may be precious, but not every event caters to your children. Hire a babysitter and enjoy yourselves.

Training children begins early. At age 3, Natalie's first dance teacher Mrs. Jane Buford, taught them this song:

Stand up straight,

Concentrate,

Don't chew gum

and don't be late.

You know what?

You know what?

I go to dancing school!

<u>Things Mammas say:</u>

Don't be **ugly**. (This refers to behavior, not appearance.)
Stop acting **tookie**.
She's acting a little **grownie**. (Like she thinks she's grown up)
He's **too big for his britches.**
Mind your manners.
Show that you've got some home trainin'.
Put on your face. What a lady should do before you leavin' the house.
Boy, you are tryin' my patience today.
You better act like you got some sense.
Pretty is a pretty does.
Don't be telling a story! (Lyin')
Kill her with kindness — if you are having problems with a friend or enemy

<u>Some mannerly suggestions:</u>

Kids thrive with set rules. Be fun, and loving and consistent. Permissive parents often have rude children. You are the parent; so, don't hesitate to parent them.

Please don't be a "counter." Your kids will never react until the final number and the method of discipline is irritating to ~~me~~ other parents.

Saying ma'am and sir is second nature to well-bred Southern children.

Northerners, or as we call them, Yankees, think the ma'am/sir thing is sassy. It is not. It is respectful, as taught in Southern homes.

In some areas of the South children call adults who are close friends of their parents by their first name, Miss Katie or Mr. Sam. In other areas, they use the last name, as in Mrs. Bohanan. Both are correct. Just don't let your child use first name only.

Often the use of Aunt is used even when that is not the case. Aunt Nan and Uncle Brooks are actually my husband's cousin and his wife, and Aunt Tee and Uncle Billy Joe are my best friend and her husband.

When a parent hollers from another room, "Natalie!" The proper response is "Ma'am?" (or "Sir?") never, "WHAT?"

Teach your child to say, "May I use the restroom?" A bathroom has a bathtub or shower, so restroom is always an appropriate word.

Going "t-t" or "tinkle" is what Southern children say as toddlers. Never, "I gotta pee." Or, "I gotta use it."

I love the innocence of children. Once a little girl tattled that her friend used the "s" word. She had said, "shut up!"

And two children overheard fighting — one used the "f" word. "FFFffffff... fine then!"

There is a difference between "Can I?" and "May I?"

Never tell your children to shut up, and they won't use the phrase. Ask them kindly to "**hush**," and you will get a better response.

"**Y'all hush!**" is commonly heard in the South.

"Sorry 'bout that" and "my bad" are not apologies. "I'm sorry" and "Please forgive me" are correct.

"You're fine" is not a good response. Neither is "yeah."

In fact, **back-talking** cannot be tolerated. Children can express their feelings, but only in acceptable and respectful ways. Hearing, "This sucks!" and witnessing eye rollin' makes me wanna **snatch somebody by the hair!** And letting your child say, "whatever" and then walk away is a BIG mistake.

Good Southern children are taught to not use the words "fart" (**toot**), "stink," "butt," (bottom), or "hate".

When asked about a food, their reply if they don't like it is, "It's not my favorite." Gagging sounds are frowned upon.

Family "hangs back" when a meal is served with guests. Your company should fix their plates and have a seat first. This is especially true at church potluck meals — ask your teenagers to allow their elders to go first. And parents, helping the little ones makes the line move faster.

Say grace before meals. Please teach your children to sit at the dinner table until they are excused. They should be expected to say thank you, and push in their chairs.

If you solicit for your kids through Facebook, you are not teaching them how to succeed in completing a task. If you make an online appeal, it should be your child who does the follow-up. I think it's cute when the parent makes a video of the child explaining what/why he/she is selling. If you hate "selling," write a check, but don't ask your friends to buy wrapping paper "for" your children. There's a small group of your close friends your child can personally ask to buy something from them who will always say yes. An exception to this is Girl Scout Cookies. I will buy them from anyone!

Teach your children to introduce themselves. Natalie had a book called *The Little While Friends* and it helped her to understand you may just play with someone one afternoon.

Train your child to invite someone to join a group if they are alone. Never condone bullying.

Help your children to enunciate their words and look an adult in the eye when responding to a question.

Help them with anger and how to manage their emotions. I've heard, "Once is cute, twice is a spankin'." As adults, they'll have to manage stress and practice conflict resolution. Getting his or her own way in order for a parent to avoid conflict is not the answer.

Self-esteem is not as important as self-control.

Entitled children, impatient children, and rude children are often friendless children.

And please understand, though teachers constantly work on many of these responses, it is not their job. It's yours.

If your children shoplift, make them return the item. Do not make this easy on them, no matter how embarrassing or inconvenient it is for you to return to the store. Make them apologize too, and personally hand the item over. As a retired gift shop owner, I can assure you this is a learning moment. And the proprietor will be firm but kind, even if it breaks her heart.

Instruct your children to finish what they start. Quitting teams mid-season or dance lessons before the recital will lead to abandoning ventures later in life... like dropping classes or quitting jobs when they can't get the time off they want. It's just not real life.

Allow them to quit after the term or season is completed. Then encourage new hobbies. If your child is miserable at a sport, guide him/her to visit privately with the coach. Simply inquiring, "what can I do to improve" can bring a positive change to their relationship. As an adult, however, they will realize it's fine to quit a book if they're not drawn into the plot.

Indulge your children's interests. Not everyone likes ballet, soccer, gymnastics or taekwondo. Helping them find a hobby doesn't have to require a lot of money and will help shape their unique personalities. Let them study violin, bake, decorate cakes, learn to play the harmonica, make rockets, sew, or juggle. My friend Sandra's granddaughter opened a snow cone shack, and she's the youngest member of our chamber of commerce. Go geocaching as a family. It's free!

Teach your child to take turns and to share.

Help your child to learn appropriate interactions with friends who have disabilities. Your friendliness and positive reactions will teach acceptance to them. And children are taught to see color. Show them your acceptance of all races and religions.

Bored children have been overexposed to fun. As parents, you have work responsibilities. So, teach your children that they can just play, or read, and not be entertained.

Teach your older kids not to ride their bicycles on the sidewalk.

Little girls are given a lot of leeway, especially from their daddies, but they are taught at an early age to keep that bow in their hair!

Let children learn first-hand the difference between winning and losing. Taylor couldn't help but still keep score in a "friendly game." He was just competitive. But we taught him to accept a loss with dignity. If children hear adults talking about the refs or umpires, they will feel justified to complain. Watch yourselves. Your children won't be successful at everything in their lifetimes, so help them learn to accept defeat. And when playing board games and cards at home, there's a time to let them learn and a time to beat them. You'll know.

Teach them how to answer the phone by identifying themselves.

Help them learn to keep their feet off the furniture. (Insert laughter, as the twins think my couch is a jungle gym!)

Teach them how to write thank you notes. Just sit them down, hand them a pen, and have 'em do it. Then teach them how to address an envelope and where the stamp goes.

As a child of the 60's we knew to be "seen but not heard". When my parents entertained, we were introduced to the guests and then scurried upstairs to play until bedtime. With "couples friends", the kids are very much present nowadays. But this is a reminder to young parents that it is okay to have adult time. Please understand that not everyone enjoys your child trying to be the center of attention.

To be specific, parents, teach your children not to interrupt when adults are talking. When being introduced, they should respond, "Nice to meet you." And, respond when spoken to.

Require your older children to never close the door to their bedrooms when friends are visiting. And it's a good idea for daughters to understand that boyfriends aren't allowed in their bedrooms.

Teach your sons hat and cap etiquette. (see p. 136)

If you put down your phones and other devices when spending time with others they will learn from you. And as the parent, you can insist that they do so. Teens must understand how social media can **come back to haunt them**. If they wouldn't want their mama to see it, they shouldn't be posting it.

Teenagers benefit from a good understanding of generosity, respect for others, self respect, humbleness, the importance of responding to an invitation, dressing appropriately for the occasion, good posture, good hygiene, being courteous, listening with interest, and how to politely decline a food they do not like.

Show them in your daily routine, how to introduce themselves, shake hands, give up their seat as needed, and to speak to those present when entering a room.

Also, as guests at their grandparents or at sleepovers, they should keep their towels off the floor, make the bed, and be helpful to adults.

Teach your children by example. Don't spit out your gum, except in a napkin to be placed in a trash receptacle. Never litter.

Teach them to help carry in the groceries. Show them how to let others off of an elevator before trying to get on.

Insist that they throw away their own trash.

Kids should understand consequences.

Help them learn the meaning of delayed gratification.

Show them how to save money.

Teach them about networking and how the people they meet in life will have a direct impact on future opportunities.

Help prepare them for **big church**. Quiet toys, writing in the bulletin, and M&Ms help.

Teach them to hold a door, or open a door for others. Teach them the mantra, "Every door, every time".

Teach them how to use a napkin and put it in their lap. Teach them how to hold their silverware correctly. They should learn to chew with their mouths closed, and to not talk with food in their mouths.

Ask them to only comment on someone's appearance if it is a compliment. And teach them how to give a compliment. Most people think of compliments as concerned with appearance. But complimenting someone's laugh, their heart, or their personality means so much.

Ask them to knock on a door before opening it.

Train your children that if they break something, to always **fess up**. It is much kinder to apologize and be forgiven than to hide it and feel bad. In our home we said, "Come clean and tell the truth." We had several pool cues and light fixtures broken over the years and it was truly "no big deal."

Children should be taught to push in their chair — at their desk at school as well as at the dinner table.

Cultivate your child's concern for others. Being first is not nearly as important as stopping to go back for the person who is struggling to make it to the finish line.

Cover your mouth when you yawn.

Kids can't help but try to get to spend the night if they are having fun together. You can handle that delicately depending on the circumstances.

Restrict screen time and video games. Your children are a pleasure and a delight if you train them to be. Being socially present means having lively conversations, knowing how to play "I spy, with my little eye...," and being able to ride in a car without a watching a movie or using a tablet. We did it, and so can they.

Teach your kids what a "pinky swear" is.

Oh, and teach them to never double dip!

And remember, they'll never be too old to be tucked in at bedtime.

Prom

Dear Parents,

Please teach your children some manners. Prom isn't just about the dress/tux/limo. It's about how to behave in public, how to treat your date like a lady, how to meet her parents, and how to be the envy of all the elders who see you out that evening. At one point in gathering information for this book, I put out a Facebook appeal for the worst etiquette faux pas people had witnessed. Behavior of teenagers on prom night was a hot topic. The fellows wearing sneakers or ball caps with a tux is tacky. Girls taking off their shoes or having chipped nail polish is tacky as well. All of this reflects on you, parents.

Prom is an initial introduction to proper behavior in public without their parents. The limo ride and dinner should include some positive expectations about being gracious to the server and not being rude in public. You wouldn't want someone from your church to say anything to you EXCEPT how attractive and well behaved your children were, so take the time to give them a little training. Also, a prom dress is not the opportunity for your 16-year-old to dress **like a hussy**. A good Southern girl knows leaving something to the imagination is much more attractive. Help her select a dress that is appropriate for her age as well as her figure.

Sincerely,

Cindy Smith

What to Avoid Saying

Southerners are bad about getting into other folks' business.

Recently married couples don't like to be asked when they plan to start a family. They may choose to wait several years, or they may be having difficulties. They may not desire having children at all.

Also, when a couples' pregnancy terminates in miscarriage, saying, "It's God's plan" is not a kind response. I believe God doesn't intend for bad things to happen, so this will not placate the parents. Just tell them you love them and are so sorry.

Same with single folks. They hate being asked, "Have you met anyone special?" Or "How's your love life?' Most have not, if you haven't already heard. Taylor will really give me a hard time for this section of the book, because naturally I was notorious for asking just that.

The good news is that well-bred Southerners answer our inappropriate questions in a kind manner and just move on.

Gentlemanly Behavior

A few thoughts about Southern guys:
They are particular about their steaks, their bourbon, their music, their beer, and their music.

They typically carry a pocketknife.

They love their mommas.

They walk girls to class, and into church, and think nothing about holding doors and paying.

Fishing is an enjoyable pastime, as is college football, hunting, and knowing everything about classic American cars.

But if you need a few reminders, here are the right and wrong things a guy can do. And trust me, a kind gesture doesn't go unnoticed.

There is a whole generation of boys who don't know to remove their hats. To their parents, "Shame on you!" If you are in a building, uncover your head. Whether it's a hat, cap, or toboggan, take it off.

My husband still fights me on this. If he's in a casual restaurant and sees any other men with hats on he doesn't want to take his off. He used to want to leave his hat on because his hair was messed up. That is no longer a problem as he is mostly bald now.

Always remove your hat during a flag ceremony and during the singing of the national anthem. It goes without saying that if you hear that song, cover your heart. If you aren't patriotic you must not be Southern and there is no hope for you.

Never wear a hat during a prayer.

Keep your hair and facial hair tidy and trimmed. Wooly beards are humorous to me — seeing the guys with beard covers in Sam's Club. On the right guy, I think man-buns are super sexy.

Tattoos are a form of expression, but "not my favorite". For both men and women, visible tattoos CAN possibly close doors.

When Taylor went away to college I taught him two things:

To keep an umbrella in his car for a date

To know how to open a bottle of wine

His granddaddy taught him how to tie a tie. My husband taught him everything else.

Leave your phone in your pocket. Your date is more important than anything else going on during your time together.

Don't cuss in front of the ladies. That goes for spitting, too.

Follow through on whatever you do.

If you look someone up and down, it's best to follow with a compliment.

Never ask a lady her age, or ask a woman if she's pregnant.

Stand when introduced to anyone, and stand when a lady enters the room. "A lady should never be left standing alone." Hold the door. Open the door.

Say grace.

Have a firm handshake, and offer it often. Never shake hands while seated. When in doubt, always stand.

Don't **dig in** (to a meal) until the hostess begins.

If the food in a restaurant is bad, do not berate the waitress. She didn't prepare it. Kindly ask to have it returned to the kitchen and specify what is wrong.

Try to remember specific details. If you can remember all the plays from a football game, why can't you recall the details about a baby's birth? Oh, that's right, you weren't paying attention.

Women do not care what KIND of snake it was. IT WAS A SNAKE!

Please put the toilet seat down.

Walk closest to the street when on a sidewalk with a female. This originated many years ago, to keep a lady from being splattered by a passing carriage. Don't walk ahead of her. Help her with her coat.

When leaving church, take a step back when leaving the pew and let her go first. (Don does this, and it is so sweet.)

When following the hostess in a restaurant, the lady should go first and you should help seat your date, wife, or mother. Pick up the check, especially on a first date.

When seated at the table, if your date excuses herself, or the hostess (while dining as a guest in one's home) rises for any reason, it is polite to stand as they depart and return.

When you drop someone off at home, wait until they get inside before driving off. If you are on a date, walk her to the door.

Avoid the humble brag. Do not talk about money. Exhibit honesty and integrity in everything that you do.

Don't enter the pool by the stairs or other guys will ridicule you.

Never be too big to do the small things.

Return a borrowed car with a full tank of gas. Use your turn signal.

Always wear a suit and tie to a church wedding, and a funeral.

About that jacket — the middle button should always be closed. The upper one depends on your mood. The lower one should never be closed.

About that tie — the tip of it should just touch the top of the belt. Never shorter, not too long. Practice until you get it right.

And unless you are Elder West, if you are wearing a shirt without a jacket, you don't need a tie. Refrain from ever wearing a tie with a short sleeve shirt.

In the summer, a Southern fella looks dapper in a seersucker or linen suit. I love a guy in Bucks (shoes). Southern gentlemen love pocket squares and can often be seen sporting a bow tie. Ties and pocket squares should not match, but complement each other.

Southern guys don't wear factory-distressed jeans. Years of wear gives denim that true worn look.

As to everyday dress, if you tuck in your shirt, you should wear a belt. Your belt should be the same color as your shoes. So match those leathers.

Your socks should be long enough that when you are sitting your naked legs don't show.

Ask her father for her hand in marriage.

Ask your daddy to be your best man.

Sincerity is a necessity. An exception is if a woman asks if she looks fat. It's not enough to say "No!" You must also act surprised by the question. Jump backwards if necessary. (Not original)

Provide strength and support to those you love.

When you're wrong, admit it. When you're right, be quiet.

Value family and the traditions your family has provided. Be loyal to and protect your loved ones. You can tell the size of a man by the size of the things that bother him.

If you are a guest in someone's home, or my son visiting for the weekend, offer to take out the trash. This is an act that will always be appreciated. And if you see someone returning from the grocery store, by all means, leap to your feet and help carry the bags into the house. Thank you.

Treat a lady as you would want your daughter to be treated.

I like this saying:

Teach your son to be a gentleman. Train your daughter to accept nothing less.

Chivalry is not dead. Make deliberate considerate gestures and they will not go unnoticed. When you take a girl out, wash your car first. And yes, we like to have our door opened. And when you arrive at an event, it is "oh so considerate" to let her out at the door before you park the car. She can wait for you just inside, instead of having to walk across the parking lot.

Classic cowboy boots are a Southern staple. Know how to dress them up and you can wear them just about anywhere. Yes, in the South, especially Texas, cowboy boots are acceptable footwear.

My husband wore Sperry Topsiders all through college and they came back into style early 2000s. When he discovered Merrells he fell in love. Natalie had to find him a pair of "dress" Merrells (if that's even a thing) because the suede was sometimes too casual. He wears tassel loafers with a suit.

Men have it pretty easy. Do these things and you will be considered a gentleman... unless you talk with your mouth full, belch, cuss, etc. But did I really have to say that?

Make your momma proud.

I loved the sitcom called *The Middle.* If you somehow missed this show, find it on reruns. The character Mike Heck says every man should know how to do seven things:

Tie a tie.

Whistle with his fingers.

Read a paper map.

Grill with charcoal.

Shine his shoes.

Open a bottle without an opener.

Break down a door.

Not sure about the last one, but you never know.

Vin Diesel said, "Being male is a matter of birth. Being a man is a matter of age. But being a gentleman is a matter of choice."

Examples of Gentlemanly Kindness:

Once when floating the Mulberry River, my husband and his canoe partner (a novice) **tumped over** numerous times. They lost everything, including the beer, and it was a Sunday. Some college boys, who were obviously **raised right**, collected several of the beers downstream and paddled upriver to return them to the guys.

In high school, my friend Frances and I had a tire blow out nearly four hours from home. It was our first solo trip to the University. The man who did the repairs took us to his home to wait, where his wife offered us something to eat and drink.

Keep a Lady Happy

Southern girls are gracious and kind, unless you make them angry. We may throw a **hissy fit** or **fly off the handle**. Avoid seeing us **pitchin' a fit** at all costs. I absolutely **lose my mind** when told to "shut up." In the South we say, **Please, hush**. If you hear of a lady **havin' a come apart**, you'd best apologize ASAP. And **havin' a conniption** is the very worst. Just saying.

Carryin' on is crying or **makin' a fuss.** Stern looks can sometimes curtail this activity in children.

Having a **come to Jesus meeting** refers to setting someone straight.

Losing your religion means you internally or actually cussed someone. An example would be, "When that guy cut me off in traffic, it made me lose my religion."

Losing your manners, on the other hand, is slang for passing gas. Do not confuse the two.

Rednecks, Good Ol' Boys and Po' Trashy Folks

Yes, there is a difference. Rednecks are good old boys; comfortable with their guns and pick up trucks, but respectful of their mommas. Most every Southerner has a little redneck in them and is able to laugh at themselves. That's why Jeff Foxworthy made it big.

We can all easily sing along with Garth Brooks' *Friends in Low Places.*

Southern, Country, and Redneck are vastly different. Peckerwood is an older phrase, but refers more to financial shortcomings.

But nobody wants to be considered **trash.** Trashy folks are lazy, lack respect for others, and receive little respect from others. And note that being poor doesn't make someone trashy. The **"Po'"** means pitiful. Money, or the lack of it, doesn't enter in to their chosen behavior.

Poverty is a condition of wealth, not cleanliness, manners, education or class.

Trashy folks put their broken-down cars up on blocks in the front yard, right near their grill. They leave their lawn mower out right where they left it to go grab a beer. They haul their old couch out onto the front porch, too. (Can you imagine the critters that could move into an exposed couch?)

And they think **beatin' someone's ass** is the answer to any disagreement. Fighting it out physically versus intellectually is their way.

Their kids talk back to their teachers while their parents are trying to figure out a way to get on disability. The whole family can be found wearing pajama pants at **the Walmarts**. They flip cigarette butts out into the parking lot on their way in.

The guys call their wife or partner their **ol' lady** and their children's mother calls him her **baby daddy**. Just no.

People are considered trashy when they "air their dirty laundry" on Facebook.

Front yards should be appealing to your guests, pleasant for the neighbors, and complimentary to your community. I cannot get over people who leave all their kids' toys and their ice chests out in the front yard.

Gossip

This is good: Gossip always reveals more about the gossiper than it does about the gossiped.

I've always found, that if it is your friend, there is no satisfaction in hearing gossip...only sorrow, or concern. However, if the person is merely an acquaintance, gossip can be entertaining. That's why it is best to rethink gossiping. It can cross lines and damage friendships, and be considered bullying.

If an acquaintance asks you about something delicate concerning a friend, learn to say, "It's not my story to tell." That's a lovely way to avoid exposing another's shame, guilt, or hardship.

There are so many quotes about gossip to help us refrain from doing it.

Gossip dies when it hits a wise person's ears.

People won't gossip in front of folks they know won't participate.

No gossip, no regrets. Words that soak best into ears are whispered.

When you are wrong, apologize. He had to **eat crow** means he apologized.

And if you're ever the center of a scandal, do your best to bear your misfortunes with grace.

My mother taught me that the more you say, the guiltier you appear.

The best thing to do is pause. Being a "blurter" is, unfortunately, part of who I am. That's why I love going to church. I love forgiveness, and being reminded of Christ's patience and grace. So, it's a good idea to pause before assuming, accusing, and judging others.

In our small town, the community embraces those in need and obliterates those who have crossed the line. Big gossip is typically affairs and divorces. I have no sympathy for a mistress. I've heard, "If they'll do it with you, they'll do it to you."

I have never heard my mother-in-law gossip. She is a gem.

And let me tell you... *Country Living Magazine* would be so proud to get inside her home to photograph it. Granny and PeePaw spent years traveling and going to flea markets. She has spent 65+ years gathering the most beautiful array of primitive antiques. She has collections of crockery, antique toys, quilts, rocking chairs, as well as seasonal decor. It is truly a treat to walk through her home and witness her labor of love. Her home has always been welcoming and interesting, as it is like no other.

They never missed a single event that my kids were involved in. I love my sisters-in-law, Susela and Glendela. They call me Cindela.

Traditions We Shouldn't Let Go

Knowing your neighbors
Whether you just wave or have block parties, it's a gift to know your neighbors. This is especially true for us if a tree falls, (we have tremendous trees) or when a dog runs off.

Baby books
My kids love theirs. You can't keep it all on your phone, so take a little time and preserve/collect those memories.

Handwritten recipe cards
Now that my mom has dementia, there are thousands of things I wish I could ask her. Your family's recipes, complete

with smudges, will mean the world someday. So write yours down for your children.

Before Natalie got married I passed out recipe cards to all of the ladies in our Church. She has a whole file of their favorite recipes, all handwritten.

Last year she asked Granny, my MIL, to write down her dressing recipe. Then Natalie had it made into dishtowels she ordered from Etsy, and gave them as Christmas gifts.

Writing important dates in the family bible
Tracing a family tree is sure easy if you own the family bible.

Love Letters
I have one from my grandfather written before my grandparents were married. In it he talks about how someday their grandchildren will fly to visit them. I found the letter in the 1970s and they had been married in the 20's. Hard to imagine.

Addressing adults
Well-bred Southern ladies and gentlemen know to talk to the hosts or chaperones at any and every party or reception. They are guests, and they know to show their appreciation by having conversations with not only those who invited them, but with any elders in the room.

Modesty
A Southern lady covers up. Leaving more to the imagination is more appealing. There are the girls you date, and the one you bring home to meet momma. Remember that.

Calling instead of texting a friend
We have all experienced that a lot is missed or misunderstood by not actually talking.

Asking a person what they preferred being called (May I call you "first name?"), learning and remembering their name, and looking at them when speaking are such kindnesses.

Photo albums or scrapbooks

Your children will wish you had more than a computer to view photos. We cannot imagine how technology will come along, but you will someday appreciate not having to search in the cloud while the photos are arranged in a book on the shelf. An example of this is that I took our VHS home movies and had them put on a DVD, and now they could be on a flash drive. Several online companies can help you easily create albums.

Small Southern town book stores featuring local authors and artists

Really, any small business or local restaurant is going to give you better attention and good service. Cookie cutter and large stores get the job done, but without the smiles and special care. And remember, the small businesses are the ones who buy the yearbook ads, donate to little league, and reinvest the money you spend, putting it back into your community.

After all, who doesn't love to step into an old country store and hear the screen door shut behind them?

Stocking a celleret

These lidded wooden liquor cabinets date back to the 1700s, marking the wealth of Southern planters and an abundance of alcohol. A bar or liquor cart is more modern, but these bottle boxes have some flair.

Wearing an apron

Besides keeping your clothes clean, it can dry tears and help insulate your hands when moving an iron skillet off the stove.

Wearing a corsage on Mother's Day

Red if your mother is living. White if she is deceased.

Things I Miss

Being able to call the local hospital to check on a friend's condition.

Having an attendant pump my gas and offer to clean my windshield.

Having a friend with a police scanner, so I know what's going on when I hear a siren.

Having someone dial a wrong number and visiting with you twenty minutes just because you give them your attention and interest.

Teens going hunting before school and having a gun rack in their trucks. And no one considers it to be unsafe.

Going spotlighting just to see wildlife. Now it's illegal because of the folks who shoot game from their vehicles and on others' property.

Part Six
Cookin' & Eatin' and Such

Y'all, we are "all about food" in the South. That's why, besides fine dining, we have cafés, truck stops, barbecue joints, and diners all featuring plate lunches and specials. We have cities that you go to specifically to E.A.T. New Orleans and Charleston come to mind as fabulous gourmet destinations. And every Southern state boasts some of its own amazing food.

Southern culture is expressed through our food. We grew our own food long before it was considered "cool."
We women love just to read a cookbook. When we share recipes, they are called "Aunt Betty's Pound Cake," or "Miss Ruby's Spaghetti Sauce."

A meal that is just downright delicious is **slap yo' mama good.**

While on vacation, my friends and I are known to discuss where to eat supper while we are eating our noon meal.

We "fix" a meal. We don't call it cooking a meal.

State fair food here in the South is a huge competition, especially in Texas where they just try harder. Funnel Cakes were invented in Pennsylvania, however, which is a huge disappointment to me, because I was just positive we had thought of them.

Roadside fruit stands are part of Southern culture. The drive to the white beaches of Destin from our house is about nine hours, allowing for potty breaks. As soon as we hit Yazoo City there are produce stands the rest of the way. I also love to see the nurseries where they are growing azaleas. To help enjoy the drive, buy some boiled peanuts.

Our *farmer's markets* have a much longer season than our northern friends. We begin selling broccoli and lettuce in April and finish the growing season with collard greens and sweet potatoes in November.

Presentation of food at a party is very important to a Southern hostess. We may use our silver, or some pottery, or vintage china, or enamelware, or woodenware. You can be sure we won't just put a piece of cheese out on a paper plate. That's not to say we don't love a Solo cup.... But they're usually for tailgating and outdoors.

We like our table to be pretty. We gather a few flowers for a vase and pull out some cocktail napkins. It's just nicer that way.

A Southern lady would rather have a gracious home than a perfect one. We want you to feel welcomed. Grandmother's pretties are appreciated and displayed, as well as used.

Deliciousness

Here in the South we have a lot of double word foods, including shrimp and grits, chicken and dumplings, turkey and dressing, peas/beans, and cornbread, and biscuits and gravy. Now, doesn't that sound good? And have you tried chicken & waffles? That didn't sound good to me at first...but it is!

And yes, we know that obesity is a big problem this side of the Mason-Dixon Line, but we're trying. We can't help that all our good social occasions revolve around food.

And in the South, we are known for occasional **day drankin'**. Elsewhere this may be considered alcoholism, but for us, **day drankin'** can mean you're having a fish fry, or enjoying an afternoon at the horse races, or spending the day on the lake, or floating a river, or having a toddy with your grandmother, or sitting on a friend's porch.

Pimiento Cheese is known as the paté of the South

I make a smoked Gouda pimiento cheese, that is divine. Pimiento cheese is good on a croissant, on top of a burger slider, or made as a grilled cheese. A proud moment for me was when my daughter (who works for Sam's Club) mentioned to the food buyer that I make SGPC. Now they make and sell it, and it's pretty good!

Pimiento cheese sandwiches are served at the Masters (Augusta National) in fairway green bags for $1.50.

Deviled eggs

Every Southerner has her own take on how to make them. They are served at every holiday and potluck meal I've ever attended.

Southern brides should have at least one deviled egg tray. I have two for everyday and a Christmas one.

Biscuits

Let's have a little talk about these delicacies. I'm talking about buttermilk biscuits. Not Bisquick, frozen, or WOP biscuits that you wop against the counter to open.

Hmmm. There are ham biscuits, biscuits and (sausage) gravy, biscuits and (white chicken) gravy, chicken & biscuits, those cheddar herb biscuits from Red Lobster, biscuits & jelly, biscuits and syrup, and the Southern favorite, biscuits & chocolate gravy. It is a homemade chocolate sauce and is essentially dessert for breakfast... but you know it's a special day when you get it. Elvis even used to eat chocolate gravy at Graceland.

Chocolate Gravy
1/3 c. unsweetened cocoa powder
3 T all-purpose flour
1 c. sugar
1 pinch salt
2 cups milk
2 T butter
2 t. vanilla extract

Whisk together the cocoa powder, flour, sugar and salt, adding the milk until the lumps are gone. Place over medium heat and cook 5 - 7 minutes, stirring constantly, until the gravy just begins to boil and thickens. Remove from heat and still in the butter and vanilla until melted.

I've never had *tomato gravy*, but it's a Southern thing, too.

148

Don likes *cathead biscuits*. Big ol' biscuits, as big as a cat's head. The secret to making biscuits is to make them quickly so the dough is cold when they go in the oven.

I recently saw that an Arkansas couple used a chocolate fountain at their wedding reception as a gravy fountain, and served biscuits to go with it. Good move, I say.

I personally like biscuits, or any home baked bread, with real butter and a little honey. Why do they even make margarine and all those fake butters?

They've proven that they aren't better for you, and they sure don't taste good. I lived in France for a while in college. Everyone ate bread with real butter everyday, and drank wine, and ate delicious food with cream sauces. You know why they weren't fat? Because the cost of food is high so they had small portions, they walked much more than Americans do... and many of them smoked. Ha!

I saw a video of a guy watching a cooking show, and remarking after a Yankee chef added broccoli to mac and cheese. I was hysterically laughing at his response to this act. "Truly, the Lawd should shun that chef for ruining perfectly good mac and cheese."

Southern-style *Chicken salad* is made of white meat only. The breast. Dark meat is more flavorful and not needed with the extras added to make chicken salad good. That's the Southern way. The younger ladies are now buying rotisserie chickens and using them for chicken salad and chicken enchiladas. It's good, too. But don't serve it at a "luncheon" with more mature ladies, or you'll get a few raised eyebrows.

Chicken salad sometimes has pecans, apples, grapes or other deliciousness added in. I like mine with egg, a little celery, a tiny bit of onion and a dash of curry powder.

There's even a new Southern franchise, Chicken Salad Chick (Auburn, AL 2015)

In the South, we eat *Nabs*. They are the cheese crackers originated by Nabisco. They are a great snack to keep in your handbag.

Big No-Nos: Instant grits, instant tea, instant coffee

Cucumber sandwiches are an essential for every afternoon reception and tea. Cream cheese, a little mayonnaise, dill, and cucumbers are delicious. Mix the cucumber and dill with a little onion and Greek yogurt and you've got taziki dip.

Cheese straws. If you haven't enjoyed them, you are missing out. A combination of sharp cheddar cheese, butter, flour and chili powder is the best flavor explosion in your mouth. I've also had cheese wafers made similarly with Rice Krispies; great for when friends stop by, or any reception or afternoon party.

Our *tea* is iced, and enjoyed year 'round. When we ask for tea, we generally expect it to be sweet. An iced tea pitcher is a necessity. And it needs to be full and chillin' in the refrigerator.

Our tea is sweet, and our *cornbread* isn't. Cornbread with sugar should just be called cake, because it doesn't need to be at my table. In fact, sugar in cornbread is a travesty.

I make my cornbread in a cast-iron skillet. When the recipe calls for oil, I use bacon grease that I have used to coat the skillet. I place it in the oven while I mix the cornmeal, buttermilk, eggs, etc. Then I pour the hot bacon grease into the bowl, stir it in, and pour the whole bowl of batter back into the skillet. "Yum" is all I can say.

And whose grandparents didn't eat crumbled cornbread in milk as a snack? A guy from Texas told me they make sweet cornbread and pour syrup on it. I can't wrap my head around that. Why not just make waffles?

Our vegetables, fruits & sides:

We know how to make vegetables fattening... and delicious. We start with a little bacon grease or a ham hock. Some cooks add a dash of sugar. Or we bread and fry our vegetables. A plate lunch is normally **"Meat and 3"** and the three can be (among other things) fried okra, mashed potatoes, dirty rice, mac & cheese or even twice baked potatoes.

We have, however, discovered Zoodles, spaghetti squash, roasted vegetables, and olive oil. So, perhaps we are on our way to healthy eating.

Okra, fried or boiled, is a Southern food. My Grampa Toby's okra stew is a hamburger, tomato, okra, jalapeño stew, and it is a favorite. I love getting texts from friends that say, "I made Grampa Toby's okra stew today!"

Watermelon Can't get much more Southern than that on a hot summer day. And thank you to the elderly black fellow who years ago taught me how to tell if one is ripe. Listen for a deep thump, and rub the skin with your fingernail.

Black-eyed peas and the *pot liquor* from greens to dip your cornbread in is a Southern favorite. You'll find them on every buffet. When they become available at the farmer's market, people will be **puttin' up peas** for many meals to come. Black-eyed peas (cooked in hog jowl) are served throughout the South on New Year's Day to have good luck in the New Year. The saying is, "For Luck and Money".

Collard Greens (or cabbage) are often also served... for profitability.

Collards are bitter to some diner's taste, but they are a Southern favorite. **Cookin' up a "mess o' greens"** is sure to get a large group to sit down at your table.

It seems that during the Civil War, Yankees thought that black-eyed peas were grown for animal feed, so they didn't destroy them. They didn't know what they were missing.

Hoppin' John is black-eyed peas served over rice, with a little bit of green onion on top.

Grits are best served baked with cheese, eggs, garlic and a dash of Tobasco. Many Southern restaurants offer grits with butter for breakfast.

Sautéed *green beans* are one of my very favorites. With or without almonds, but still crisp. I just love them.
But, you cannot find a Southerner who wasn't raised on green beans that were simmered all day long...so long that they're no longer green. We're known for overcooking and using plenty of seasoning on our vegetables.

Tomatoes

There's nothing like a perfect summer tomato. Nothing mealy and bland about a Bradley County Pink Tomato. And I love heirloom tomatoes. I'm good at growing cherry tomatoes. July summer meals are often BLTs.

Tomato aspic with a dollop (or dab) of homemade mayonnaise. Most often served at funeral receptions.

Southern Tomato Pie

Tomato and mayonnaise sandwich, a summertime favorite, always on plain ol' white bread.

Fried green tomatoes, made even better if served with remoulade sauce or a seafood topping. They're good in sandwiches, too.

Candied yams

With brown sugar and pecans, or marshmallows melted on top.

Fried taters and onions

Southern Fried Cabbage

Vidalia Onions — This Georgia favorite must be grown within a few miles of Vidalia to be considered this variety. They are sweet and mild and delicious.

Butterbeans

Rice —White, wild, brown, basmati, jasmine, Carolina gold — we love it all. We even love sushi, so there!

Cream potatoes — mashed potatoes. Not potatoes in cream sauce.

Although we do love new potatoes in cream sauce.

Chow Chow — Appalachian pickle relish that is wonderful on black-eyed *peas.*

skillet *creamed corn* or *fried corn*

Corn on the Cob — we like to call them **roantneres** (roasting ears).

Taters, mashed taters, tater salad, and sweet taters

A friend's husband said, "If you're gonna serve me instant potatoes, don't ever give me potatoes again!"

Hash brown potato casserole — Google the recipe if you've never had it. Better yet, just come to one of our potlucks.

Squash casserole

Pineapple casserole

Everyone's mamma served them *pear salad* — a half a canned pear, a dollop of mayonnaise, and a little grated cheese.

Soak salad is an Italian salad that was dressed and left to sit for a while.

Congealed salad   Lord, there are too many to list.

Ambrosia   Made with fruit, marshmallows and coconut.

Everyday dishes:

Chicken spaghetti — a staple at every fellowship meal, potluck, or funeral meal.

Poppyseed chicken

Country ham

Red Beans & Rice — the best I ever had were at Felix's Oyster Bar in New Orleans.

Gumbo — first ya gotta learn to make a roux, then this okra based soup can contain seafood, chicken, sausage or duck. Let's not forget *jambalaya* and *etoufee*.

Southern fried chicken Everyone's grandma made the best. We even have good fried chicken in convenience stores. And the competition is great for fast food franchises, as well:

Kentucky Fried Chicken (1930)

Chick-fil-A (Hapeville, GA 1946)

Church's Fried Chicken (San Antonio, TX 1952)

Popeyes Louisiana Kitchen (New Orleans, LA 1972)

Bojangles (Charlotte, NC 1977)

Raising Cane's (Baton Rouge, LA 1996)

Slim Chickens (Fayetteville, AR 2003)

Chick-fil-A, or as my grand-twins say, "Chick-da-flay" is a marvel. The atmosphere is friendly and the Chick-fil-A sauce is "a party in your mouth!" I'm not lyin'. It's so yummy they keep in it the back. I'd be tempted to fill my purse if they kept it out. Proud that this company chooses to close on Sundays.

Chicken fingers — at the University of Arkansas, (Go Hogs!) the Greek System has "chicken finger Friday" when everyone invites their friends to the house for lunch.

Chicken fried steak and gravy

Fried pork chops

Southerners love a good *crawfish* boil and they know what "don't eat the straight ones" means. We also call them crawdads.

Salmon croquettes — Everybody's mama made these with canned salmon on a busy evenin'.

Deep-fried U.S farm-raised catfish with hush puppies — There's just nothing quite like it. Delicious paired with *green tomato relish*. *Hush puppies* are made of corn meal and onion. They got the name because Confederate soldiers tossed them to the dogs to quell their barking.

Slugburgers — popular in north Mississippi and the surrounding area. Created during the Great Depression in Corinth, Mississippi, these deep-fried burgers are easily found in greasy-spoon diners.

Tur-Duck-Hen — Turkey stuffed with duck, stuffed with chicken, then roasted to perfection.

Bacon

I know bacon isn't entirely Southern, but we are big fans. Just about anything is made better with bacon. We even make candied bacon, baked with brown sugar and served as finger food. We call it Pig Candy.

Frito chili pie

Pickled pigs' feet — can't actually say I've tried them.

Chitlin's — this either!

Southern Pies:

Pecan pie is a holiday favorite. We say pa-cahn in Arkansas. In some Southern states, they say p-can.

Sweet potato pie

Buttermilk pie

Chess pie

Black bottom pie

Vinegar pie
Custard pie
Peanut butter pie

My mother-in-law makes a *cracker pie.*

Fried pies — made with either a pastry or doughnut type dough, with chocolate or fruit fillings, these delicacies can be found throughout the South in cafés, quick stops, and bakeries. They're called hand pies in some areas, but those are baked, I believe. Some savory flavors are being offered now.

More desserts:
Bread pudding

Must be moist; raisins are optional, but get my vote; and should be served with a bourbon or vanilla sauce. I once shared bread pudding with a friend at every meal on a weekend trip to New Orleans. I don't regret this activity one bit.

Nanner puddin'

Nilla Wafers originated in New Jersey but they are most definitely a Southern staple. If you wanna stay all-the-way Southern, buy Jackson's Old-Fashioned Vanilla Wafers. Banana puddin' is just good, y'all.

Bananas Foster

A New Orleans specialty that I really could make at home. But half the fun is watching it flame up at your table and being served the warm bananas and rum sauce over homemade vanilla ice cream.

Peaches & peach cobbler

"Elbow peaches" are the peaches that are so ripe and perfect the juice drips down your arms. It's best to always only buy peaches in the summer. They are hard as bricks when they are out of season, and they never ripen to taste good.

Chocolate cobbler
Blackberry cobbler
Hummingbird cake
Italian Cream Cake
Caramel Cake
Coconut Layer Cake

Coca-Cola cake — chocolate sheet cake made in a jelly roll pan, with or without pecans in the icing. Yes, Coca-Cola is the secret ingredient. Buttermilk, too.

Beignets — a NOLA fave of fried dough and tons of powdered sugar. Delicious after a late night enjoying New Orleans' jazz.

King Cake — This Louisiana specialty is sold in bakeries throughout Louisiana during Mardi Gras/Carnivale season preceding Fat Tuesday (the day before Ash Wednesday). The cakes are a ring of twisted cinnamon-roll style dough, topped with icing and sugars in purple, yellow and green. The tiny plastic baby placed inside comes from the holy day of Epiphany when Jesus was first seen by the three wise men. The tradition is believed to be brought from France in 1870. The baby symbolized the Baby Jesus, and brings luck and prosperity to whoever finds it. That person is responsible for bringing the cake the next year.

Our obsession with pickles:

Fried pickles with Ranch dressing.

Whole *pickles* — sold in concession stands throughout the South.

Koolickles — You heard it right...powdered Kool-Aid poured into a jar of pickles.

Wickles Pickles — They are sweet/hot. Buy some.

Our Sandwiches:

Po boys — in Maine they make a lobster roll. In the South we like to put fried shrimp or fried oysters in a French bread sandwich.

Muffulettas —Buy one at Central Grocery in NOLA — that olive salad on top is life-changing.

Fried Baloney Sammiches

Odds 'n ends:

Hoop cheese from a country store, a pocketknife, and a sleeve of Saltines — best picnic snack ever.

Spoon Bread — a cornbread soufflé-type casserole

Hoecakes — or *Johnnycakes* — cornmeal and water/milk, eggs, honey, or butter, long ago cooked over a small fire on the hoe's blade as a meal when working in the field.

Pecans — roasted & salted, or candied with brown sugar, butter, and a dash of cinnamon

Muscadine jelly

Mayhaw jelly

Pepper Jelly — a hot blend that is delicious served on cream cheese   See also: *Pickapeppa Sauce*

Benne seeds

Sometimes known as sesame seeds, these aromatic seeds make the richest buttery wafers. A Charleston favorite.

Viennies — canned Vienna Sausages. Potted meat.

Fried pork rinds — found in any convenience store. But absolutely delicious cooked fresh in trendy restaurants.

Rotel — Simple to make at home cheese dip, made using another Southern staple, Velveeta "cheese".

My mom used to make open faced grilled cheese toast with a slice of bacon on top. She would put it in the broiler and...yum!

Everyone agrees that cheese dip made with a box of Velveeta and a can of Rotel can feed a big group of teenagers. If made with two cans it's a little runny and is scrumptious served cold while floating a river on a hot summer day. Somehow, food always tastes better when you're outside.

Natalie says the most Southern thing I've every said she overheard at a tailgate when I said to my friends, "Have y'all seen the price of Velveeta lately?" (Really, how can fake cheese be so expensive, and so good?) Either way, Velveeta, cream cheese, and cream of anything soups are staples in Southern pantries.

When we ask for a **coke**, we may not want a Coca-Cola. We may actually want a Sprite or a Dr. Pepper. We don't use the words soda or pop.

There's a drive-in in Helena, Arkansas, with a sign that says, "Best Coke in town!" That's referring to the ice and size of their fountain drink, because it's not necessarily Coca-Cola.

A cold, bottle of *Coca-Cola with a sleeve of salted peanuts* poured right in is a Southern delicacy.

Cheerwine — a cherry-flavored (non-alcoholic) soft drink produced in North Carolina continuously since 1917. Never tried it, but I will when I get the opportunity.

Grapette grape soda, manufactured for decades in Camden, Arkansas

Southern Candy

(Many Southern candies contain pecans and peanuts.)

Divinity

Goo-Goo Clusters

Blue Bell ice cream

Chick-o-Stick

Pralines

Bourbon balls

Turtles

Peanut Patty

Peanut Brittle

Moon Pies

Little Debbie cakes

Dippin' Dots

Air Heads

Boudin

When I was a naïve 20-year-old, my parents let me spend a semester in the suburbs of Paris as an AU PAIR (nanny). It lasted until the husband came on to me, and I abruptly moved into the city. It was a wonderful experience, nevertheless, meeting people and immersing myself in all things French — the culture, cuisine, arts, food and wine.

One food that I couldn't tolerate was Boudin Noir, which is sausage made with pig blood. Seriously, I can still remember how truly disgusting it was.

Many years later I refused to eat Boudin in Louisiana, because I thought it was the same thing. It isn't. *Cajun Boudin* is stuffed with rice, onions, peppers, and pork. It can also contain crawfish or alligator. It is delicious, y'all, and can be found in Jambalaya, another delicious dish.

Andouille sausage is smoked pork sausage, another Cajun favorite.

FYI, Miracle Whip may be sold in the South, but it is not mayonnaise. It is tangy, and labeled a "dressing" and must be a Yankee thing. We use Hellman's mayonnaise, but Duke's (made in South Carolina) is the true Southern *mayonnaise*. There's a big following for Louisiana's Blue Plate, but homemade is best.

It was while I lived in France that I learned to make mayonnaise. Here's the recipe: (It's a pretty amazing science experiment and teaches you about emulsification. The truth is, it just takes patience.)

2 whole eggs

3 T lemon juice

1 t dijon mustard

1/2 t salt

Pepper to taste

1 1/4 c canola oil

Keeps for two weeks in an airtight jar.

(Another unique thing the French do is to flip the plate over after a meal at home, and use that small rim as their dessert plate. Oftentimes, we would stir a little table sugar into fresh yogurt and add a few berries.)

Some Southern sauces include:

Hot sauce, may be influenced by our Mexican neighbors, but we make a lot of it in the South.

Tabasco

Louisiana Brand Hot Sauce

Panola Pepper Sauce

Texas Pete (from Winston-Salem, NC)

Comeback sauce   delicious on seafood, but especially Saltines.

Remoulade for seafood.

Jezebel sauce   This is typically served with ham, and made with pineapple preserves, apple jelly, horseradish, and hot mustard.

I had quite a time learning how to cook. I like to blame it on the fact that my mom never gave me an Easy-Bake Oven for Christmas. (Sweet Daddy Don gave me one last year to enjoy with my grand-twins.) I'll admit that making a meal is not my favorite thing to do. Owning a gift store, I got HOME at suppertime, so cooking wasn't very fun. I made a few mistakes.

I made stew early in marriage and served it to my kind father-in-law. The vegetables were still hard. He never said a word until I did, and then we had quite a laugh.

My cooking today isn't quite as bad as Ellie Mae Clampit's. (Remember, they used to bury it in the backyard?)

My northern sister-in-law, Stacie, made tuna casserole the first time without pre-cooking the macaroni. She later became a gourmet cook and fabulous meal planner.

Entertaining, as opposed to just cooking for my family, is much more satisfying for me. I like to plan meals much more than preparin' them. I love selecting the menu, preparing my shopping list, and executing the meal for a group of appreciative fans.

Barbecue

Whether it's dry rub or smothered in sauce; ribs, pulled pork, or beef brisket; we Southerners don't play when it comes to talking about our BBQ. The sauces can be sweet and tomatoey, or vinegar based. Everyone has his own favorite style of BBQ and each state has a dozen favorite restaurants.

Jones BBQ in Marianna, Arkansas, has James Beard award winning barbecue. He sells out by 11 a.m. each day. My friend, Kim, will be so proud I mentioned Mr. Harold.

Hoots BBQ in McGehee, Arkansas, has put our town "on the map"! Shout out to Susie and Hargie from #specialneeds

The Rendez-Vous in Memphis should be on your bucket list.

I like dry rub BBQ with a vinegar based sauce. But pork slathered in sauce is pretty good, too.

Yankees call *cookin' out* or *grillin' out* a "barbecue". Barbecue is the FOOD to us...what we are eating. This is a cultural difference no matter which side you're on. Barbecue is not a VERB. What I'm sayin' is, don't invite us for barbecue and serve hot dogs. That's just called a get together.

Equally important as getting together to grill is the fish fry and crawfish boil. There's just nothing so good as Southern fried farm raised catfish and hush puppies; a crawfish boil with corn, sausage and potatoes; or a Low Country shrimp boil.

Southern Cocktails, and alcohol consumption

Southern spirits and an early evening toddy are important to our lifestyle.

Besides sweet tea, Co-Cola, and bourbon, other popular Southern libations include:

milk punch — a no-egg eggnog, made with bourbon

bloodies — and we like 'em hot and with a skewer of fancy veggies

Southern Planters Punch — a rum, lemonade & sweet tea, and mint concoction

Mint juleps — and serve 'em in the julep cups, please.

Jack & Coke

Muscadine wine

Coffee punch — strong brewed coffee, milk, vanilla & chocolate ice cream, sugar and whipped cream

New Orleans Sazerac

Margaritas

West Texas Ranch Water — Topo Chico mineral water, tequila, and lime juice

And to go along with **day-drankin'** these are often available in a "go cup" when you head out to your next event. Natalie had a mimosa one morning before leaving to go to the horse races. She fixed a **to-gosa** for the car ride to the track.

My friend Alicia invited a group of ladies for brunch. She served three types of mimosas, identified with hand written signs:

Presbyterian mimosas were made from a frozen orange juice, pineapple juice and amaretto slush with champagne added.

Methodist mimosas were champagne and orange juice.

Baptist mimosas were just orange juice.

In the South, we know the difference between having some drinks, and **havin' some dranks!** The latter is much more fun. My friend Sarah uses the phrase, "I've gotta go drink about it!" when she's in a conundrum.

I'm not a big fan of straws. I just prefer drinking from a glass. But in a mixed drink, are those itsy-bitsy straws actually straws or just stirrers? Well, I did some investigating, and cocktail straws are actually there for a reason. They allow you to take small sips from your drink and not over-imbibe. However, if you are drinking from fine drinkware, simply remove the straw, as they can be pesky.

Frosé is super popular now (though not reserved for the South) — rosé wine frozen with strawberry simple syrup. "Frosé all day" as the saying goes.

A *road pop* is a large beer, usually consumed still in the paper sack.

And let's not forget *moonshine or white lightnin'*. We could've used this for hand sanitizer during the unfortunate Coronavirus of 2020.

BTW. Did you know Louisiana still has drive-thru liquor stores where you can pick up daiquiris? They literally have veeeeerrrrrry liberal open container laws in their parishes, which the rest of us call counties.

When a Southerner is "over-served" he/she may be:

all to' up
drunker 'n Cooter Brown *
knee walkin' drunk
He was bad to drink
Shit-faced
Three sheets to the wind

* Legend has it he lived on the Mason-Dixon Line and had kin on both sides. He decided to get drunk and stay drunk to avoid going to war.

Lagniappe

This is a Louisiana term for "a little somethin' extra". A lagniappe is something given as a bonus or extra gift — like when they throw in a couple of donut holes when you are buying donuts.
— or when you come upon a band playing music when you're walking through a quaint little town.
— or finding a selection of cookies and coffee served in your favorite boutique
— or being served cold water cornbread when you are seated in a restaurant

An *amuse bouche* is a treat that you didn't expect, given by the chef. They are served gratis and according to the chef's selection alone. Don't think, "Well, I didn't order this!" — just enjoy!

The first time I was served an *amuse bouche* was at the Biltmore Inn in Asheville, North Carolina. This French term is not exclusively Southern. It translates to mean "happy mouth."

Afternoon Tea

I love "taking" afternoon tea. I've enjoyed tea at the Biltmore Inn, the Plaza Hotel, numerous Chicago hotels, the Empress Hotel (Victoria, British Columbia) and at Harrod's in

London. Tea is a wonderful way to rest your feet after shopping or touring a museum. I appreciate the ambiance as well as the fare.

Tea can actually be considered somewhat of a ceremony. The finest silver, porcelain and linens are used. There is an art to the presentation and taking of tea.

There are a few rules to enjoying afternoon tea:

Try to avoid making any sounds with your spoon while stirring the cup. Then place your spoon at the top of your saucer, never on the tablecloth.

If your tea comes in a tea bag, do not put it on your saucer. Your server should provide you with a small dish. This dish is for your strainer, as well.

Lift the saucer and the cup together when drinking tea.

Never place the slice of lemon into the cup. The heat and rind will make your tea bitter. Just gently squeeze the lemon, and set it aside.

Spoon the clotted cream, curd, or jam onto your plate. Then use your silverware to prepare your scone.

Slight extension of your pinkie is correct. Please do not exaggerate this practice or you will look pretentious.

When serving tea, the oldest lady present is served first, then the other ladies according to age. Then the gentlemen are served in the same manner.

A teakettle will bring the water to a rolling boil. Microwaving the water makes lousy tea because the molecules don't heat evenly. (The things I've learned in my "extensive" research!)

At the Grocery Store

Oh, the drudgery of going to buy supplies, shlep them home, and put them up. Natalie is a big fan of using the pick-up service, but I still like to pick out my own bananas.

A good Southern lady knows a few tricks to make her day a little brighter. We greet people and stop just to chat. When getting a buggy, we give one to the other person waiting on one. We help older people get items in their buggies and their bags into their cars. We hold the door for others. Try it, and your day will be brighter.

The most important rule at the grocery store is the kindness of letting someone go in front of you if they just have a thing or two. Really, what's it gonna hurt if you give them a minute of your life? I'll bet it has happened to you. You walk up to find a buggy FULL in front of you, and the customer graciously waves you in front of him/her to keep from waiting. It's such a gift... and one you should return when possible.

There's another thing I've watched Southerners do well. If there are four or five people in line and another line opens, we look to person #2 and indicate they can move. We don't peal off the back (like they do up north), racing to the register. What they do even makes more sense, but our way is just kinder.

Also, if you just walked two miles inside the supercenter, you can walk another ten yards to put your buggy up. Sometimes your feet have reached the breaking point, but it is a courtesy to not leave your buggy to roll into your neighbor's vehicle or block the parking space. Don't be the person that abandons a buggy.

Kindness, folks.

Things stupid people do:

Take more than the allotted number of items to the quick check line.

Eat grapes and bananas in the produce section...also known as shoplifting.

Talk on the phone during checkout, or on speaker mode within the store. (Don't y'all know we're supposed to be visitin' with the checker?)

Block the whole aisle by parking on one side and standing on the other. (Hand up, here, as I forget and do this occasionally.)

Take toddlers to the grocery store during naptime or late at night and then yell at them for being cranky.

Decide against purchasing a frozen or refrigerated food and abandon it on a random shelf.

Pull money out of their bras. SBM (sweaty boob money)

Part Seven
Why Are There So Many Rules?
(But I just gotta cover everything!)

Cellphone Etiquette and Digital Decorum

I am about to point out some specifics — but friends, this whole book is about being mindful of others.

Never speak on your phone in a restaurant or movie theater. Your phone should be SO on silent that you don't even know anyone is calling. And in a restaurant, just excuse yourself and GO OUTSIDE.

Do not place your phone on the table next to you in a restaurant. (Yes, I do this occasionally. Is it okay? No.)

Do not text or check your phone in the theater. That screen in bright, people.

Obviously, turn it off for church, a funeral, concert or play.

No call or text is more important than the person you are with.

I will admit that when my sister-in-law and I join our mother-in-law for supper, we often use our phones to share pictures with her. She doesn't do Facebook, so she loves to see the current pictures. Then I often have some printed for her.

At work, you are being PAID to interact with the customer. Or, you have a job to do WITHOUT distraction. My employees would ask, "Well, what if someone needs to talk to me?" I'd say, "They can call on the work phone and if you're not busy with a customer, you are welcome to speak with them."

Walking through a store while talking on your phone is ~~rude as hell~~ thoughtless and unkind. You are distracted, and it is difficult for the staff to approach you. And please don't check out at a store while on the phone. You delay the process and it's frustrating to the people behind you.

Parents, please teach your children to speak clearly and to identify themselves on the phone. We didn't grow up with caller ID, so we know to state our name. Just like they have no idea what "long distance" is, they don't know to identify themselves. Please teach them how to apologize and be kind if they misdial as well… as opposed to just hanging up.

Telemarketers take advantage of older people who learned phone etiquette. They were taught to be polite and carry on a decent conversation. Even with caller I.D. a call looks like a local number. Hang up. It is no longer considered rude.

It is always nice to ask to be excused and step outside when making or receiving a call.

If someone shares a photo with you from a phone, it's ~~tempting to scroll and see more pictures~~ polite to hand the phone right back after looking.

If the Presidential motorcade goes by, by all means use your phone to snap a photo. But if you are at a wedding, your phone better be in your bag or pocket… on silent. The couple has hired a photographer, and the last thing that they want is:

a. You being the first to post photos from their ceremony.

b. Their **expensive-ass** professional pictures to show the guests with their phones in the air instead of enjoying the moment.

I went to a Bruno Mars concert and realized my friend and I were ~~old~~ on the older end of the spectrum when all the kids were taking selfies with him in the background. That was a great show.

My favorite artists are all "aging out" — The Eagles, Earth, Wind & Fire, Fleetwood Mac. So, I had to find some younger singers/bands. Ed Sheeran was fabulous in concert. I just want him to come hang out one evening and sing with my friends. I'm sure he'd love our Southern Hospitality.

I once witnessed an infant baptism where the grandmother's best friend was all over the church trying to capture the moment. First of all, she was not a professional and didn't have that manner the professionals have of somehow not being seen. Secondly, she kept stopping the pastor and trying to get a pose. Good Lord, why couldn't she just wait until after church and get a posed photograph then?

Please honor the sanctity of the Covenant of Marriage and the Covenant of Baptism. Carry memories in your heart. They don't have to be photographed or videoed.

Dating

Don't dumb yourself down for a boy. In fact, never play dumb except at the poker table.

A lady wants to be cherished, and appreciated, so be yourself and make your mama proud. Pretty is as pretty does, is what your grandmother told your mama.

Don't be convenient. My mom taught me to never accept a date for the same day.

Don't meet him for a date — have him pick you up. When I was in college, I loved being picked up for a date at the Tri Delta House. Don came into the foyer and called my room. All the other girls greeted him, but his smile was reserved for me. The feeling of descending the curved staircase was inflating.

Being walked to the door at the end of the evening was special, too. Then came cell phones, and groups of girls flocking to the fraternity houses, and I don't think my son ever experienced picking a girl up at the house.

Many years ago, there was an awkward guy who married a girl who was, shall we say, not from his same background. She was, as we used to say, "easy." My friends and I coined the term, "She flung it on him," which is pretty self-explanatory. He never knew what hit him. The marriage didn't last.

Bless my daughter for patiently living through all the talks I had with her about "protecting her virtue."

In the chapter room during *rush*, which is now called *recruitment*, we were allowed to say, "QR" if a girl had a questionable reputation. It was acceptable to be concerned that she may direct her energy more into her social life than her grades and the benefit of the house.

Ladies, when you get into a car, sit down first and swing your legs in. There is a right way, and a very wrong way, to exit a car in a dress. You'll avoid hitting your head on the roof, as well as flashing passers-by.

Going Dutch vs. having him pay — If he asked you out, a Southern guy intends to pay. Let him.

If you read much these days it seems like this generation has made it seem like a man being loyal to a woman is a luxury, when in fact it should be a standard.

Online Dating

I know this is a thing. Please, just be careful.

And for this, do meet in a common area, and let your friends know what you are doing. Gosh, I'm old fashioned... but, still!

My Mimi passed away at age 81. She was priceless and precious and a joy in my life. She was the first person with whom I shared these thoughts. She didn't think she was too old for new things, so we bought her a laptop, then later simplified her life with an iPad. She loved being connected with family and friends on Facebook, looking at Pinterest, and perusing new recipes. She had a friend who met a man online and they married. When I asked about her, this is how Mimi described it, "Well, she got her one of them Internet boyfriends. She drove to Missouri to meet him and decided he got a pretty good check. So, she married him. But I think now she's a little disappointed he's still alive. She's stuck taking care of him." I laughed so hard I had to pull the car over!

Breaking Up

Ghosting is when one party just quits responding and basically disappears. This is cowardice.

Never break up by text or phone call. Or email. It's cowardice to end a relationship in public. The best location would be to do it at the home of the rejected one. It starts with four simple words... "We need to talk."

Sexting

I am big on texting. It accomplishes the job. It doesn't irritate my husband while he listens to music in the car, as a means for me to communicate with friends. After all, our phones serve as our cameras, GPS, calendar, weather source, calculator, flashlight, and so much more.

But when did someone decide sexting was a good idea? Case in point:

A local coach was trying to get back with his wife whom he had apparently disappointed by having an affair. He was going to church again to try to fix things. Then he got the idea to send her a pic of his "package." He had been part of a group text with his Sunday school class... and what did he do? You guessed it. The hilarious conclusion to this is that he attempted to deny it by saying his grandfather was playing with his phone at the nursing home.

#1 No one's PaPaw knows how to work the camera on an iPhone.

#2 That PaPaw's privates looked mighty "young."

Sometimes ya just gotta laugh!

Netiquette

So, have you figured out that Facebook can create stress? There's always some keyboard crusader out there attacking people's posts and stirring things up. If you give your opinion, be prepared to be attacked. Or be prepared to have an open mind. Just be prepared... because no one ever "wins" on Facebook unless you post something funny/embarrassing about yourself, or pictures of cute baby animals.

Office Etiquette

Basically, be considerate and respectful of others.

Be on time for work and early for meetings. Respect others' time.

Have a firm handshake, both men and women, and never shake hands sitting down. Look people in the eye.

When meeting with someone you met previously, reintroduce yourself using a point of reference from your last meeting. For instance, shake hands and say, "I'm Cindy and we met last March at the conference."

Answer emails promptly.

Praise co-workers when they have done a good job.

Don't take credit for another's work.

If you do a favor or kindness for others it will not go unnoticed.

Stay home if you aren't feeling well.

Keep your phone calls quiet as well as your phone sounds.

Leave the communal kitchen tidy. If you drink coffee, make coffee.

Try not to eat foods that have odors that are offensive to your coworkers.

Don't over-share about your personal life.

Listen without interrupting.

Dress appropriately and conservatively.

Do not criticize your competitors to your customers.

Wear your nametag on your right breast so it is easier to see when extending your hand for a handshake.

Exit the elevator to let others in and out, rather than blocking the entrance.

The custodian and mail guy deserve your respect as much as the boss.

Participate in office donations, never calling attention to the amount you give.

Business Dining Etiquette

Arrive on time and introduce yourself.

Don't drink with customers or at least follow your company policy.

Don't ask for a to-go box at the conclusion of a business dinner.

Turn off your phone.

Never assume your client is looking for a social encounter.

If you initiated the meeting, you should always pay.

Proper Introductions

There are all sorts of rules about who to introduce first; whether one is older or younger, male or female. But the simple fact is that it is rude to have a conversation with someone with your friend or spouse just standing by. Just simply say, "Bob, this is Tamara. Tamara, Bob"

My husband panics when he cannot remember a name. (Why is it that your mind goes blank at the most inopportune times?) I've finally just gotten him to say, "You remember my wife, Cindy?" And hopefully they'll say, "Yes, I'm Thomas."

And it's okay to just introduce yourself.

One thing that frustrates me is being introduced over and over to the same person. Maybe I'm not memorable. It's always kind to say, "Good to see you again," if you're not quite sure.

Do not confuse this with the retort, "Oh, we've met." That's Southern for, "I remember you were horrible to me, but you don't remember because you can't admit what a horrible person you are!"

Just Plain Rudeness / Common Courtesy

I don't like to listen to other peoples' phone conversations in a public place. No one does. Nor do I like to listen to their music. Please keep your conversations and phone calls quiet and

---

172

don't blast your music in public. Headphones are for the music. But, I still don't want to hear your side of the conversation. For the love of God, step away before I have to give you "the look."

Please don't litter. Take it home and dispose of it there.

If you live in a city, pick up your dog's poop. For this, and many reasons, I'm glad I live in a small town and our dogs have a lot of room to play.

Earlier I asked you to use your elbow (or left hand) when you cough or sneeze. The right hand is the one you use to shake hands. And speaking of handshakes, a firm handshake is mandatory. Not bone crushing, but firm. For ladies, as well. You're not extending your hand to be kissed. A gentle but firm handshake is correct.

Your mama taught you that whispering is rude and she was right. So is allowing your daughter to tell secrets.

Your mama probably mentioned that you shouldn't point at people either. If you do gesture, use your full hand.

This is a delicate issue, because at the time it is impossible to correct:

Guests shouldn't bring guests. If the hostess has an event planned and her guests show up with people she doesn't know, it not only throws off the numbers but can change the whole atmosphere of the party. Don't drag a friend along or invite someone because you know she'll have fun, too. It's simply "not done."

Remember this when taking your children with you to a coffee or shower. The hostess may not be prepared for restless children looking for a playroom. Once again, check the envelope. If your children aren't included in the address, get a sitter.

A good friend was recently the MOB as her daughter got married. The mother had one guest call to ask if she could bring her sister. I guess she thought she would enjoy it. Never mind that she was obviously not on the guest list.

Another guest texted the mother of the bride a photo of the dress she bought for her daughter to wear. Her daughter, whose name was not on the invitation. Goodness gracious.

———

Chewing ice doesn't get on my nerves. But it gets on other people's nerves, so don't do it except in private. Remember teaching your kids not to slurp their milkshakes? Same thing.

We give a helping hand to strangers.

Southerners, whether man or woman, hold the door open for the elderly, disabled, or anyone within a few feet of the door.

It's not old-fashioned to give up your seat... to parents with children, pregnant ladies, the elderly, and the disabled.

It's not about first come, first served. It's about putting others' needs before yours; and sharing a smile, too.

And how kind is it when ladies rise when another, older woman, enters the room? It's just so respectful and courteous.

A few forms of **common courtesy** include:

Resetting the weight machines to a lower setting at the gym when you are finished.

And wiping up your sweat.

Replacing the toilet paper roll.

Being quiet in a movie theater, and putting your phone away.

Not standing too close to the person in line in front of you.

Not driving too slowly in the passing lane.

Help Out a Friend

It is not rude to let a friend know she has ~~a booger~~ the need to wipe her nose. Just wipe yours and she will usually do the same. Spinach or pepper in your teeth, or lipstick on your teeth, can be similarly alerted by simply pointing to your mouth. I would much rather have a friend tell me, than to discover it hours later.

Once I found a gummy bear stuck to my crotch (from holding a customer's daughter in my lap to read her a story) while waiting on someone many hours later.

I've also managed to wear two different colored shoes. (Anyone else have navy/black issues?)

A simple, "Your fly is down" will help a gentleman, and the conversation can easily continue. I just realized there's literally NO WAY I could say this to a man unless it was my husband, son, or brother!

Please alert your girlfriends if they have red wine "wings." My witty Natalie coined that term.

Part Eight
Celebrating all things Southern

Southern Mamas

Southern mamas are a unique breed. We mind your business, but it's out of love, not criticism.

When you are young, their job is to prepare you for adulthood, and to love you. The rules are important. So is having fun. That's why vacation planning and birthday parties are left to the creativity and desire of mothers.

We like details... like growing our own mint just outside the kitchen door, just for iced tea. Or having a spot for everything... in the desk, the pantry, or the junk drawer. After all, y'all depend on us to find everything.

We are known for "calling the roll" when we are angry. In searching for your name, we may call out the names of all of your siblings and dogs first. But you know eventually your name will be said, and we mean business.

We're good at multitasking. We can feed the dogs, unload the car, check the mail, and pull a few weeds, just on our way into the house. We have exemplary attention to detail. We keep up with social engagements, gifts to buy, parties to plan, and which bathroom is running low on toilet tissue. We are precise with everything except our age and weight. Actually, I'll proudly announce my age, but the only time I tell the full-out truth with my weight is when the snow ski rental guy needs to know how tight to adjust my bindings. This gal doesn't want to tumble down the mountain unnecessarily!

Things mammas threaten:

I brought you into this world and I can take you out.
You better hop to it, missy.
You'd better straighten up 'cause I'm fixin' to jerk a knot in your tail.

I'll slap you into next year!
You need to nip that in the bud. Stop that behavior immediately
I'm gonna pop the fire outta you. Spank
Stop that, or I'm gonna pop ya upside the head. I'd like to pinch your head off.
Do you want me to go cut a switch?
　　　　(Or worse, she'd send you to get it.)
Go get ya a switch! — before ~~you got yo' ass to' up~~ tannin' **your hide.**
I'm gonna tell your daddy!
You are tryin' my patience.
Do you want me to pull this car over?

Long after you're grown, mamas remember your favorite meals and traditions, and, want your childhood home to be a refuge for you from all the responsibilities of life. We are quietly courageous and our love for family knows no bounds.

Hanging out with your grown-up kids is like visiting the best parts of your life

— Unknown

Daddy

Daddy's girls are common in the South. Not just because daddies love and spoil their daughters, but because they recognize what is special in a little Southern Belle. They can often be heard telling their daughters to be sweet and mind your mama.

They work hard, they play hard, and their love of family is ferocious.

Sons learn from their father's example by how he treats others. Childhood is so brief, but the bond is everlasting.

Her daddy will be the standard against which a daughter will judge all men.

Things fathers say:

Mind your mama.

You'd best get glad in the same britches you got mad in.

Measure twice, cut once.

Shut the door.

Quitcher belly achin'.

I'll give you somethin' to cry about.

Please look me in the eyes when I'm talkin' to you.

Love you, sweet pea/son.

Things Unique to the South

How Southern are you?

Put a check by all that you've experienced/seen.

___ The Peabody Ducks

___ Enjoying the Mighty Mississippi River: it's just a trickle up North.

___ Paddleboats. They may have them elsewhere, but the lower Mississippi River is where you'll keep an eye out for a classic.

___ Seeing kids cardboard slidin' on the levee.

___ Levee ridin', ridin' backroads and turnrows, and bonfires. This includes drinkin' alcohol and/or lookin' at wildlife.

___ Tubin' — slowly floatin' down a river in an inner tube with a beer in your hand on a lazy summer day.

___ Searching for crawdads in the bayous and ditch banks.

___ We don't buy mistletoe at Christmas — we shoot it down.

___ Sipping ~~nectar~~ **the sweet** from honeysuckle blooms.

___ Taking your cast iron skillet with you on vacation (and knowing just how to care for it).

___ Wild mimosa trees blooming pink in the summer.

___ Pulling cicada shells off pine trees and sticking them onto your t-shirt (or crunchin' 'em with your foot.) Hearing their song at dusk.

___ Frog giggin' and eatin' frog legs.

___ Cotton gins, cotton bales, and memories of playing in cotton trailers.

___ Fishin' with a cane pole, a jug, or trotline.

___ Seeing a horse in a stall at Sonic... because, the Sonic ice, y'all!

___ One-stop stores — You can peruse antiques, use the tanning bed, have your lawnmower repaired, and buy some boiled peanuts, all at the same country location.

___ We love monogramming all our pretty things. From julep cups to pillows, rear car windows, towels, bags, children's clothes...we are pretty creative.

___ The importance of being a legacy in the Greek System.
    Sororities and fraternities are different in the South. They just are. Fellowship, honor, respect, and support are words that describe the Greek system. Modern movies that portray a negative side must be made up north, because we Southerners carry a pride of those years. The lasting friendships and networking never stop.

___ The sound of green tree frogs:
    I need to tell you about Clempsey. When Don was a boy, his daddy taught the three boys that the tree frog on the window each evening was named Clempsey. So that's what Don taught

our children. They are pretty commonplace in the summer, because flying insects are attracted to the light in the window and they can catch their supper. Greeting Clempsey was an evening ritual at our house.

___ Magnolia trees, the Grand Dame of the South, and the fragrance the blooms provide each May.

___ Live oak trees. They are truly majestic.

___ Spanish Moss. This parasite hangs from cypress and live oak trees in the lower South.

___ Attending a party with a fishing boat or canoe filled with iced-down beer. (Credit: David Bonds)

___ Seeing a guy jump out of his truck at a stop sign to retrieve a beer from the cooler in his bass boat.

___ A shrub with "switches" just outside the kitchen door.

___ Weekend gun shows.

___ Having a pet squirrel or raccoon.

___ Blue Laws (stores don't sell liquor on Sundays).

___ Dry Counties (where liquor is not sold).

___ Cypress knees — the roots of cypress trees stick up out of the water.

___ Swamp-tour airboats.

___ Dill pickles and pickle pops sold in the concession stand. (Available now at Sam's Club: Fried Pickle Dip)

___ Wiped out the grocery aisles at the mere mention of a storm. You can never have enough milk and bread during an ice storm. We'll call off school for any pending inclement weather.

___ Bottle Trees — with blue bottles to catch the haints, Morning sun would destroy the spirits.
     The history began in 1600 BC in Africa, Egypt, and Mesopotamia. The practice was brought to North America when the slave trade began in the 17th Century.

___ Pecans

___ Know someone who has attended a snake-handlin' worship service

___ Hurricanes — you may have had one to drink (Pat O'Brien's) or survived one (the weather kind)

___ Eating fish on Fridays (It's a Catholic thing, but respected throughout the South)

___ Unique road kill, including 'possoms and armadillos

___ Big ASS beers
     They may be offered elsewhere by now. But, I'm pretty sure Bourbon Street in New Orleans in the first place that had 'em.

___ Kudzu — grows up to a foot per day. Also referred to as "the vine that ate the South."
     This invasive plant was declared by the USDA to be a common weed, and later a noxious specious.

___ Riding your bike and chasing the mosquito sprayin' truck

___ Huge roadside crosses, and banners praising God, hanging on the side of buildings

___ School paddlin's

___ Alligators, snappin' turtles, and alligator gar

___ Snappin' beans, stringin' beans, creamin' corn, and shellin' purple hull peas until your fingers are sore and your hands are purple.

___ Swamps, bayous, salt water marshes, the Everglades, and bogs...and mountain creeks

___ Post-high school football game on-field prayer

___ Roadside produce stands and fireworks stands

___ Saving bacon grease

___ Vacation Bible School

___ Inviting the pastor giving the blessing at an event to be seated at the head table with the guest speaker.

___ Screened-in porches — with ceiling fans gently movin' the air, and daybeds for nappin'. In the days before AC, children slept on their grandparents' screened-in porches.

___ Hot boiled peanuts, the caviar of the South

___ Trash burning in the backyard in an old oil drum

___ Paper funeral fans. It's hot down here, y'all!

___ When making iced tea, adding sugar until it "feels right."

___ Coming from a small town, means introducing yourself as "so and so's daughter or son" and then they automatically know who you are.

___ At grandma's house, finding a margarine or Cool Whip container in the fridge knowing good and well that's not what's inside.

___ Your coach is also your history or health teacher

___ At Southern baby showers where games are played — all the prizes are intended for the baby, and the winners know to give them to the expectant mother.

___ Kids learn to drive before age 10 on a turn row or gravel road.

___ Respect for farmers.

Our farms are large and the equipment is costly. (And by that, I mean more than a nice house.) Being a farmer involves working the land itself, irrigation, erosion, herbicide and pesticide use, marketing the crops, adjusting to the weather, and so much more. Southerners are patient when a tractor, cotton picker or combine slows traffic, because we understand farmers feed the world.

Don comes from a long line of lawyers, but he chose farming. His family has owned the same land since 1872 and 1921, so we are part of the Arkansas Century Farm community. Don and I were named Farm Family of our county a few years back. It was definitely because of his expertise, as I've never canned or "put up" anything. We don't live on the farm — we live in town — but, contrary to the teasing, I DO know how to get there!

___ Seeing an alligator in the wild

___ Seeing a man who ran out of gas for his truck in the driveway, driving his ridin' lawnmower to the gas station to buy some gas

___ Prison bands — it's okay to get out of the "pen" for a few hours if you can sing or play the guitar at a small festival

Our parties:
> Mardi Gras
> SXSW
> The Kentucky Derby
> Talladega
> Bonnaroo
> NOLA Jazz Fest
> Memphis in May
> King Biscuit Blues Fest

State Pride

Please add anything I've missed, in the margins.

Mississippi: (pronounced MIS-sippy)

We start here because the crooked letter state has always been "The most Southern place on earth"
They even have their own way of counting: One Mississippi, Two Mississippi, Three Mississippi...
Caramel cake
Comeback sauce
Soul Food
Kibbe — a Lebanese delight
Birthplace of Elvis, B.B. King, Oprah, Jimmy Buffet, Faith Hill, and a whole lot more, and authors, too.
Hot Tamales
Catfish farming
Birthplace of the Blues
Sweet Potato Capital of the World (author Jill Connor Browne)
The scenic Natchez Trace Parkway

Arkansas:

Lakes and rivers — We're not called The Natural State for nothin'!

The Ozark and Ouachita Mountains
The Cycling Hub of the South
Diamonds — Crater of Diamonds State Park is the only place on earth you can mine for diamonds and keep what you find
Crystals
Birthplace of Johnny Cash, Glen Campbell and Al Green
Bowie knives and bb guns
Whetstones for sharpening knives
Fried pickles (and don't forget the ranch dressing)
Rice farming
Birthplace of potpourri (Heber Springs, AR 1982)
Cheese Dip (and Texas, we're not talking about queso)
Ducks (because we're in the Mississippi River Flyway)
Walmart/Tyson's/J.B. Hunt
Ivory Billed Woodpecker sighting (And I believe it, too!)
Louisiana Purchase
Esse Purse Museum

Louisiana (pronounced LOOZ-i-ana):

Creole and Cajun cooking
Shrimp & oysters & boudin
Mardi Gras — and all things included —parades throughout the state, beads, the king cake, and finding the baby
Beignets dusted with powdered sugar
Bread puddin' with bourbon sauce
Pralines
Creole mustard
Crawdads — crawfish, also called mud bugs
Pirogues — Cajun canoe
Roux — the base to every Cajun sauce
Cane (sugar) syrup
Jazz
The Brennan Family and several famous chefs
Drive-through daiquiri stores
Bourbon Street/ NOLA/ The Big Easy
Second Line Parades where bystanders join the parade to keep enjoying the music

Hot sauce, which they believe can be added to absolutely everything
Voodoo dolls
Parishes — what they call their counties
Hurricanes from Pat O'Brien's

Alabama:

Known as "the Heart of Dixie"
Lucky state to have Sweet Home Alabama written for them by Lynyrd Skynyrd, and none of the band members were even from there.
Montgomery is the birthplace of the Confederate States of America.
The mullet toss — toss the fish over the Florida state line
U.S. Space & Rocket Center
Helen Keller
Motorsports racing — Talladega Superspeedway
White barbecue sauce
The Unclaimed Baggage Store
Muscle Shoals Sound Studios
Birmingham — named after Birmingham, England, the "Magic City" is known as the "Pittsburgh of the South" because of its iron and steel production.
Mobile — birthplace of America's original Mardi Gras (1703)
Home of Honey Boo Boo and Mamma June. (Lol. Had to throw that in because we're just so glad she's not from Arkansas.)
The beaches of Alabama are referred to as The Redneck Riviera

Georgia:

Peaches
Peanuts
Pecans
Vidalia onions
Brunswick Stew (St. Simons Island)

Stone Mountain
Birthplace of Cabbage Patch Kids (Cleveland, GA, 1983)
Augusta — Home of The Masters
Savannah Bee Company
Coca-Cola (Atlanta, 1886)
Waffle House and Chick-fil-A
Hostess Ding Dongs & Twinkies
Bulldogs
Where the Appalachian Trail begins
Paula Dean and her butter-lovin' self

Kentucky:

Bourbon Trail
Bluegrass Music
Hot Brown Sandwich — originated in Louisville at the Brown Hotel
Birthplace of Abraham Lincoln and Loretta Lynn
Beer cheese
Big Ass Fans (That's a ceiling fan, y'all.)
The Derby
Horse farms
Mint juleps
Lexington — horse capital of the world
The concept of Farm to Table began here in 1775
Bacon and pig raisin'
Burgoo — a spicy meat and vegetable stew
Louisville Slugger baseball bats

Tennessee:

Elvis' Graceland
Gatlinburg, Dollywood, and Casey Jones Village
Smoky Mountains
Music Scene —
Nashville/Music City USA

Grand Ole Opry (live radio since 1925)
Beale Street in Memphis
Aretha
Whiskey
Krystal burgers
Captain Rodney's Boucan Glaze — order it online, or find it in smaller gift shops, and win "best dip" at your next event.
Davy Crockett
Chattanooga Choo Choo — first a train, then a song, then a train station, now a hotel.
Ark Encounter (Williamstown, TN 2016)
Little Debbie Snacks
Cracker Barrel restaurants (Lebanon, TN, 1969)
Piggly Wiggly — "The Pig" was the first true self-service grocery store (Memphis, 1916)

The Carolinas: North 'n Sawff Caka Lackey

Blue Ridge Mountains
Low Country
The shag — state dance of S.C.
The outer banks and their beaches
Haint Blue ceilinged porches and doors — belief that spirits can't pass through water; or some believe it reduces insects and birds because they think it's the sky
Grits (S. Carolina)
Shrimp & Grits
Joggling boards — unique to Charleston and the Low Country, these benches are long and narrow and provide a slight bounce.
Pepsi-Cola (New Bern, N. Carolina 1896)
Moonshine
Charleston Tea Plantation
Asheville, NC — The Biltmore House
Winston-Salem, NC, 1937 — Where Krispy Kreme donuts were invented. Who doesn't love to see the "Hot Now" sign turned on?
Wrought Iron artistry
Sea Island red peas

Carolina gold rice
Sea turtles
Palmetto trees
Sweet grass baskets
Boykin Spaniels
Tobacco
Mt. Olive Pickles (They even have a New Year's Eve pickle drop)

Virginia:

Virginia is for Lovers and is known as "the Birthplace of a
Nation"
Virginia was an original Colony that went with the South during
the Civil War
Jamestown Settlement, Colonial Williamsburg
Pineapple obsession — hospitality — good tie to Southern ways
Country cured ham & red eye gravy
Oysters and soft-shell crabs
Tobacco
Virginia peanuts
Monticello and Mount Vernon
Blue Ridge Mountains
Shenandoah National Park/Skyline Drive
The Pentagon
Arlington National Cemetery / Tomb of the Unknown Soldier
Home of the U.S. Navy's Atlantic Fleet
Wild Ponies

Texas, The Lone Star State:

Everything's bigger, especially hair
The women love their bling, whether it's their jewelry or their
bedazzled clothing
Oil
Longhorns/ ranches
Music scene in Austin
Bluebonnets

Blue Bell Ice Cream
Line dancin' and the two-step
Cowboy boots
Frozen margaritas
Buc-ee's convenience stores
Brisket
Tex-Mex
The Alamo
Fort Worth/Cowtown
Six Flags over Texas
Armadillo

Florida: The Sunshine State

Is Florida even Southern? Because they don't serve sweet tea there. Just sayin'.
We love Disney World.
One reason y'all aren't as Southern is because of all the Yankee retirees and snowbirds. But at least if we get them to the South they have the opportunity to learn our ways.
The everglades and alligators
Key West
Oranges
St. Augustine — oldest city in America thanks to Ponce de Leon
Best beaches in the South
Daytona International Speedway
Lily Pulitzer
The Flora-Bama — great roadhouse/bar located right on the line. Try a bushwhacker, don't miss Big Earl, and come back on Sunday for their church service.

Oklahoma:

Y'all aren't in the South. Sorry. You're good people, and we don't blame you for wishing you were Southern.
Thank you for introducing us to the Tiger King, which proves there are rednecks everywhere. Best entertainment we could've ever hoped for during the Covid-19 shutdown. That, and Tik Tok.

Missouri:

Same with y'all, Missouri. Y'all are just too Midwest. (But we're claimin' Mark Twain because of the Mississippi River.)
How 'bout we just call y'all "honorary Southerners?"

Music and Story-Tellin'

A big part of our culture is music. That's why the Blues and Country music are so popular with us.
These genres describe love, heartache, and family.

> The South is the soul of this country.
> – Trace Adkins

I love 70s Soul and Motown. What Twilla calls some good **belly rubbin' music.**
Gospel singin' is unique to the South. Bluegrass, Jazz, Zydeco all are Southern. Don't forget Rock-a-Billy.
And the places we go to enjoy music are part of our culture — dive bars and honkytonks.
Don and I introduced our children to a mixture of James Taylor, Raffi, Queen, and Jimmy Buffett when they were toddlers. When Taylor and his best friend Garrett wouldn't participate in music, their kindergarten music teacher, Alicia, finally got them to sing along to *We Will Rock You.*
Every Southerner gets happy when we hear *Sweet Home Alabama, Strawberry Wine*, and *Black Water.*
We love storytelling. Sitting around a campfire, the dinner table, or on the front porch recounting tales of the past is a true and satisfying form of entertainment. We also enjoy tellin' a few harmless tall tales.
A longtime farmhand is often the topic of many of our family tales. We call them Oliver Stories.
"**Going to Dukey**" refers to using the restroom
"**Lay him down.**" Refers to hunting a buck
"**I got glad too soon!**" Refers to if something doesn't go as planned.

If he couldn't fix something, he'd worry it to death, or he usually repaired it with some type of wire.

"I believe I can," was his response when asked to complete a task.

He had a brother-in-law named Kitty. Oliver once shot one of his sons. The police just let it go.

Vergie was Don's grandmother's maid. She was a wise and kind woman and Grandma's true friend. And boy could she cook.

"You sho' right, ol' miss," was how she answered Grandma Gould.

She also said:

"Killin' doves is a sin." They is blessed birds. They brought the olive (branch).

Drunkified (My friends and I often use this word she coined.)

Defrosted the cotton   Defoliation of the plants before picking

Sick wagon   Ambulance

Grandma Gould had two dogs named Ruff. Vergie called them Russ and Russ, Jr.

Mortal T cat — Maltese (gray) cat

Vergil said, Mrs. Crozier went to the psychologist in Little Rock because she had to **" have her mind qualified."**

Literature

Not to brag, but our nature of storytelling has produced some amazing Southern writers:

William Faulkner

Eudora Welty

Carson McCullers

Harper Lee

Mark Twain

~~My friend, Kim, named her cat~~ Shelby Foote.

Willie Morris

We'll even claim Ernest Hemingway, since he wrote in Arkansas and in Key West.

I love books by Southern authors. Whether they are funny or recall a Southern childhood, I soak them up.

Fannie Flagg, Rick Bragg, Greg Iles, John Grisham, Julia Reed, and Pat Conroy are some of my favorite authors.

Rick Bragg (from Alabama) talks about selective morality: Never lie or steal. But some people believe it's okay to hunt without a license, or to kill more than your limit on doves or ducks in a day. Don, however, is a die-hard rule follower where hunting is concerned.

Reading is a passion of mine. I mark my pages, and get them all water-crinkled from reading in the pool or bathtub, because a book becomes a part of me. I get transported to another time and place when I'm into a good book.

And do y'all ever get a book hangover? Sometimes it takes a few days to get over the influence of a good book. Another quirky thing I do is put down a book right when I am nearly finished, because I simply don't want it to end.

Would you like a few feel-good book recommendations?

The Accidental Salvation of Gracie Lee by Talya Tate Boerner

No Back Doors by Charles Graham and Darrel Campbell

#FeelFreeToLaugh by Jordan Baker Watts,

Can't Make This Stuff Up! by Suzannah B. Lewis

Miss Hildreth Wore Brown by Oivia deBelle Byrd

Southern Lady Code by Helen Ellis
        "I'm not in charge" is SLC for "They're doing it wrong!"

Sean of the South by Sean Dietrich

Southern Architecture

Visitors are drawn to the South because of our architecture. We've got gorgeous antebellum homes, from the Greek Revival style of the Rosalie Mansion in Natchez, Mississippi, to Oak Alley in Louisiana. The coastal homes are elevated — sometimes on stilts and often on raised foundations.

Double balconies, deep verandas, and wrap-around porches are still built on Southern houses, just for visiting and enjoyment. But, they were a necessity before air conditioning was available. We love screened-in porches, too.

Shotgun houses, dogtrot homes, and Southern Colonial homes are unique, but my favorite is the Charleston Single House. The homes appear to be only one room wide, with a door directly on the street. But the door leads to the lower piazza (porch) and the actual entry midway down the porch. The two-story homes face the garden and coach house with access to the sea breeze. Walking along and peaking through the wrought iron gates is a wonderful way to discover the city.

Part Nine
Livin' in the South

The Mason-Dixon Line

It is still used today, in the figurative sense, as a line that separates the North and South politically and socially. I guess it serves as a cultural boundary

The term Dixieland is used in reference to Dixieland Jazz.

The Mason-Dixon Line started as a resolution for a border dispute between Pennsylvania and Maryland in the 1760s, but included the unofficial extensions separating free and slave states prior to the Civil War.

Patriotism

We may not have been happy to lose the War Between the States, but we love America.

Southerners fly Old Glory with pride.

We pray and sing the National Anthem at ballgames, and we don't threaten to move out of this beautiful country when we don't agree with every single person in government.

Praisin' God and Sundays (and Wednesday Evenin's)

For Southerners, religion is an easy subject. We quickly ask new acquaintances, "What church do y'all go to?" Or, "Have y'all found a church home?"

You don't hear Southerners talk about our "spirituality." We just come out and say we love Jesus, and we pretty much go to church regularly. It's not a big deal. It's just how we were raised. After all, this is called the Bible Belt.

When we give directions, the proximity to a church makes the direction-giving easier. For instance, "It's just down from the Methodist Church past the old doctor's office." is an acceptable phrase.

Billy Graham and Martin Luther King both came from the South.

We've got a bunch of televangelists, too. But, I'll stick to the two preachers who are the most respected and revered. We call 'em **preachers** instead of "pastor" or "reverend," and **Brother** is commonly used.

Y'all, I just love my church family. I go to church because it makes my week better. The love we share, the opportunity to give thanks, glorify God... it just makes me happy.

I'm Presbyterian, so we like to talk about love, forgiveness, and Grace more than guilt, damnation, and the end of time. My faith gives me strength, and my love of the Lord makes me want to live as well (and with kindness) as I can.

My faith comforts my heart. His mercy gives me strength. I live with gratitude for his life and resurrection. It's that simple.

I'm not a worrier. I pray often and try to lighten my burdens by sharing them with God. I read once that worrying is like sitting in a rocking chair... it doesn't get you anywhere. I have also read, worry is the misuse of information. I inherently think people are good, too. I like my happy bubble, and that's where I plan to stay.

History is what it is and the South has progressed. There's a lot of talk still about prejudice and racism, but it only further divides people. I read our church history where the Session discussed what action should be taken if a black person, couple, or family came to worship. This was in the early 60's. The unanimous vote was to welcome them, so let THAT be in a movie portraying the South.

Thank goodness, and contrary to what movies portray, we are allowed to dance in the South, AND read the funny papers on Sunday.

I will admit that the church prayer list is sometimes a good source of gossip. That's when you'll hear the phrase, "Bless her heart." But we actually say a little prayer, too.

In the South, we say "Merry Christmas!" because that's the holiday many of us celebrate. But we are respectful of other's beliefs. Political correctness won't keep us from celebrating Jesus' birthday.

Singin' a Special is when you have a soloist.

I cannot sing well, but I lift up a joyful voice during worship.

I love little country churches with **dinner on the grounds** (potluck after worship) and annual Easter egg hunts.

A revival is planned to get lots of folks up to the altar and **Saved** —Bringing folks to Jesus while having several days of uplifting messages. Also called an **altar call**.

A revival may have an **all-night gospel singin'**.

A **love offering** helps to pay for a special speaker, a soloist, or to help a family in need.

A **homecoming** is a special Southern gathering that brings together friends, family, and church members who have dispersed across the globe. The event reconnects them over worship and a special meal.

See also, **Homecoming** for football, bringing alumna together.

Funniest thing I ever heard a pastor say.

"I finally bought a funeral plot the other day. Never really gave much thought to dying and being buried. Just thought one day I'd be **raptured on up** to be with Jesus."

And we all love the joke about how Baptists refuse to acknowledge you if they run into you in the liquor store.

When someone is frustrated, they'll say, "They were so slow rakin' the yard it'd **make a preacher cuss**."

Backslidin' is when someone has quit coming to church and gone back to his old ways.

Gettin' right with the Lord refers to someone embracing his faith after falling away due to disbelief or bad choices.

Funerals

Ladies should own a black dress, or one in a respectable/subdued color, (for at least two seasons) to wear to a funeral. Please teach your daughters, no sequins, rhinestones or bare shoulders. I've been to funerals where college girls arrived in stilettos and their little black dresses. Uh. No. It's not a date, it's a memorial service. Please dress modestly.

Immediately after hearing of the demise, send a sympathy card. Even better to share your condolences is a hand-written note, on personalized stationery, with a fond memory or trait you admired in the deceased.

These new Facebook and online remembrances quickly escalate into a competition of who knew the deceased best. Better to share your love and memories with the family, I believe.

Send a houseplant, or an arrangement of flowers to the church, funeral home or family home, depending on the local custom.

Attend the visitation to have the opportunity to help the grieving family. Northerners call this the "viewing."

The ripple effect — you never know how you influenced the life of the deceased. Attend the funeral out of respect for a life well lived.

There will be an unspoken committee of friends who will meet friends at your door, remember who brought what, and stand at your sink washing dishes until everything is clean and tidy.

Pull over and stop for the funeral procession — any funeral procession. Just pull over and wait. It's called courtesy. I definitely think this is a Southern thing and it is such a kindness. Some people get out of their cars, take off their hats, and put their hands over their hearts. That just makes me smile. There has been some question about whether to pull over on the freeway.... do it the Southern way and just sloooooooow way down.

Pallbearers play just as an important part in a southern gentleman's funeral as in his wedding. There are those who actually help carry the casket and those who are provided a special pew in the sanctuary. Honorary pallbearers are often the older friends, if the deceased is older himself.

Take food to the house. Feed the family at the church. Good Heavens, that's what Southerners do, is feed people. Funeral food is some of the best. Every Southerner has a go-to dish that she is confident will be eaten, and she always has the ingredients handy in her kitchen. Mine is cheesecake or sausage/cheese bread. There's a cookbook out called *Food to Die For*. Great title.

Being Dead is No Excuse is another great one. The Mississippi authors also wrote *Somebody Is Going to Die if Lilly Beth Doesn't Catch the Bouquet* and *Some Day You'll Thank Me for This.* They will teach you about funerals, wedding, and mothers. I recommend all three.

Please people. Do not discuss what is going to be done with the deceased person's home or belongings. If the funeral plans have not yet been made I'm pretty sure the family hasn't decided what to do with grandmother's dining room table, so please don't ask.

When a funeral is running long, some folks say, he's trying to preach the departed into heaven.

What is the casserole brigade? It's the steady stream of ladies who bring your daddy food after your mama passes... just to make sure he's doin' okay. Actually, I've always heard that men who have had a happy marriage are open to remarrying.

Don wants to know what the timeline is on this without him lookin' bad. I told him he'd probably need to go on and get a date to my funeral just to help him pick out the right shirt and tie.

<u>Cemetery or Graveyard</u>?

It's easy to remember — the graveyard is in the churchyard. A cemetery is a large burial ground typically not associated with a specific church.

I've heard that up north they have to wait to bury folks until the ground thaws. In Southern Louisiana, their above ground tombs are necessary because New Orleans' water table is quite high. The tombs look like small houses, so the cemeteries are referred to as "cities of the dead." Early settlers learned that if buried in the ground, a big rain would pop the airtight coffins up out of the ground. That's pretty creepy. You can google it if you don't believe me.

What is *Decoration Day*? Invented by Southerners, it's a day in May that rural families gather to clean the graves and decorate the monuments with flowers in the cemetery. This was the inspiration for Northerners, after the Civil War, who created Memorial Day.

Southern Seasons

Summer in the South

The humidity is stifling. But, the slamming of the screen door makes us feel at home.

An evening in a porch swing, watchin' day turn to dusk, is Heaven.

I love noticing when it is "the golden hour."

Chuckin' rocks at turtles in the bayou or across the pond

Sittin' on the beach at twilight

Catchin' lightnin' bugs (fireflies to y'all from "not from around here") in mason jars. It's magical.

Eatin' watermelon

Puttin' up corn, snappin' beans, and shellin' peas

Listenin' to the sound of cicadas and the coo of doves

Gatherin' fresh vegetables from the garden

Bug spray is a Southern grocery staple. That's why we have screen doors and screened-in porches. We laugh when northerners complain about bugs in their yards. We don't even notice them. And we can recognize a visitor by the way he swats at a mosquito instead of just squashin' it.

Magnolias blooming

Fireworks stands

Fall in the South

Burnin' leaves

Friday Night Football

Saturday tailgates and SEC football

Bonfires

Dove hunts

The flash of a white-tailed deer

Winter in the South

Pickin' up pecans
Complainin' about the irregular weather
Duck huntin'
Hearing geese flying above and seeing their V formation
Kids playin' on the ice

Spring in the South

Dogwoods and azaleas blooming
Honeysuckles
Bullfrogs
Puttin' in a garden
Catchin' and playin' with wooly worms (caterpillars)

The Few Things I Complain About, Living In The South

Mosquitos and chiggers
Humidity. We called it Arkansauna, and it can be brutal.

Other personal pet peeves:

Misplaced apostrophes
Squeaky windshield wipers
A Kleenex in the washing machine
Driving through McDonald's for fries and discovering
they're not salted.
A kink in the hose when I'm watering my flowers
People who aren't proud of their hometowns.
What you call home — your state, your hometown —
gives you a sense of history and place. Be never boastful but
always proud of your roots and your experiences. Embrace your
history and who you are. People born to sophisticated parents in
metropolitan cities can still turn out to big boring ~~assholes~~
people, but your loved ones and experiences make you unique.
My son and his friend Anthony told the doorman at the Plaza

Hotel that they couldn't understand how he could live in NYC because there weren't enough baseball fields in Central Park and where would they ride their 4-wheelers?

I had the opportunity to represent Arkansas for eleven years as a commissioner for Arkansas Parks & Tourism. People constantly ask me where the best camping, cycling, fishing and floating can be found. Arkansas is diverse, with the Delta being true Southern, Fort Smith being the gateway to the western frontier, and the north border being nearly Midwestern. We have mountains and waterfalls, the best floatin' rivers, a presidential library, an amazing American art museum, and a bunch of good people.

Why does Hollywood think we don't have air conditioning in the South? Just a couple of years ago I watched a TV show about a Memphis cop and his office only had fans. Really?

And it makes me crazy to hear fake Southern accents from Hollywood actors. Ewwww. And we don't all drive beat-up pick-up trucks.

But truly, *Southern Charm* and *Hart of Dixie* are pretty good shows. One is reality TV and the other is a series... and I love Lemon Breeland. They are both absurd shows, and I am able to laugh at the premise of both.

Some iconic Southern television:
> *The Andy Griffith Show*
> *Beverly Hillbillies*
> *Evening Shade*
> *Designing Women*
> *Dukes of Hazard*
> *Hee Haw*
> *Dallas*

The Weather

What's goin' on outside is important in the South. Farmers can read the weather without the use of The Weather Channel, but they appreciate a heads up.

When Southern men gather, they first talk about the weather. Then the topic moves to football, and eventually they get onto other topics or down to business.

If a tornado is in the forecast, you can find me **hunkered down** with pillows, in our guest bathroom, while Don is standing outside watching the movement of the sky.

When it's **blowin' up a storm** it can be a bonus to a farmer hoping for rain. Or it can mean they'll have to get out and figure out how to get the water off the fields.

When Southerners say, **"The devil's beatin' his wife with a frying pan"** it means it's raining while the sun is shining.

Storms have a wonderful and unique smell. I love summer showers and the instant cool that they bring.

And we say the wind **lays**, not **dies, down**.

If it's **airish**, it's chilly and you may wanna grab a sweater.

A big, hard rain is called a **gully washer**, or a **frog strangler**.

I like the phrase, **"rainin' so hard the animals are startin' to pair up"**.

I've had a wind chime outside of our bedroom window for the 30 years we've lived in this house. When the weather changes and cooler weather moves in I can hear the change before actually looking out of the window for confirmation.

Southern states often "brag" that we can switch from heat to air conditioning (or back) in one day.

Our weather is so diverse I've been colder at spring baseball games than at fall football games.

Fall is my favorite week of the year. Don't blink or you'll miss seeing the leaves change color and feel the cooler breezes.

Our seasons are best recognized as deer, duck, turkey and dove. Or winter, spring, allergy, and football. Or winter, tornado, mosquito, and hurricane. You pick.

"I'm burnin' slap up" is a phrase you'll hear any Southerner use, and also said by women over 50 with their own personal defective heating systems.

Besides our humidity, it gets **hotter 'n blue blazes** in the South.

The **dog days of summer** refers to when the weather is so hot the dogs hide under the front porch to stay cool.

It gets so hot here in the summer that the best parking space is determined by whether or not it is in the shade, not the distance from the door of where you're headed. And oftentimes your car does even cool down before you get to your destination.

I personally prefer hot weather to cold weather. I love to be on the lake, slowly cruisin' on a pontoon boat, or as we call a **party barge**. I love the mountains and family ski vacations. But, I am thankful I don't live where it gets cold for several months out of the year. Taylor lived in Chicago and survived, but my favorite part about winter is when it's over.

Snow in the South means ice. Northerners love to laugh at us, but we are truly unprepared. We don't have enough snow plows. The ice cripples our little country roads. We like to even call off school in anticipation of ice. That way we can all start cooking and having a good time!

Arkansans laugh about the milk and bread aisles, which are stripped bare at the mere mention of ice or snow. Is everyone plannin' to make French toast, or what?

I live on the bayou bank, so true snow days are awesome. We have a slope into the bayou for sledding, or should I say "saucering?" The only other hill in our part of the Delta is the Mississippi River Levee. It is excellent for cardboard sliding in the fall, and, naturally, when it has snowed.

Pulling folks behind ATVs is popular, although dangerous. I've seen 4-wheelers pullin' a truck hood because it makes a good saucer.

So, tease us if you'd like. It may get **hotter 'n hell** down here in the summer, but at least we don't have to shovel snow and clear our windshields before we go to work.

Politics

Sorry, folks. I'm not touching this subject.

I believe we should all pray for our leaders. I believe we should exercise our right to vote. If people strive to be honest, moral, show empathy, and value integrity, the world will be a better place. Dinner table conversation is a daring place to get into a political discussion. This is not original, but I believe no matter your political party, we can all support the cocktail party.

Small Town Livin'

I've lived in the same small Southern town for the last 39 years. Small town living is the best. Everyone works together to help the purpose of organizations and their success.

Our grocery stores are not the best, however. Our produce is limited and we were the last to learn about hummus and cauliflower pizza crust. Thank goodness for Amazon for the things that aren't available locally.

Policemen will give you a second chance for running a stop sign. One time the dogcatcher just brought our dog home. He'd picked him up for **runnin' the neighborhood**. I promised we'd look into getting an underground barrier system, and reminded him I took his son home from youth group every Wednesday night.

When everyone knows one another, you have the best support group ever. Twilla and I watch television shows where someone is in the hospital with no visitors. That is unheard of in a community like ours. Taylor broke his arm playing football and the whole town stopped by the emergency room.

People know your business practically before you do! It's all good unless you have an affair. Bad news travels quickly, too.

Football in the South

Kenny Chesney's *The Boys of Fall* is a great country song about high school football. Download it and enjoy.

Nowhere compares to the South for Friday Night Lights. In small towns, there is a different attitude on Fridays, with pep rallies and tailgating and heading to the stadium.

Taylor's favorite sport was baseball, but the attention he received from the men in town when he was the quarterback will remain in his memory. Random gentlemen would approach Taylor and want to talk about the team and last week's game.

The *Homecoming mum* is a Southern high school tradition. For you Yankees, it's for the girls to wear, not a potted plant. Moms wear them with their son's number in the middle. And the bigger the better, I might add. They've gotten a little ridiculous in Texas, where "everything is bigger", but I sure have fond memories of their significance. In fact, many schools have different dress themes during Homecoming week as competition between the classes. The week culminates with *dress-up day* to honor the homecoming court and the football team, and of course, a big pep rally!

The art of dressing up for the Saturday tailgate is Southern. Our college girls don't just wear t-shirts and jeans. On many campuses, tailgating attire is Sunday best, but in team colors. "The Grove" at the University of Mississippi has probably the most well known tailgating traditions. Oftentimes, Ole Miss tailgaters boast of having silver service under their tents and hanging chandeliers. They have impressive trailer-style port-a-potties they call Hotty Toddy Potties. We had one at Natalie's outdoor wedding reception that we referred to as the port-a-palace. Guests even mentioned how impressive it was, in thank you notes I received later.

I've heard of weddings during a big rivalry game with men wearing ear buds during the ceremony. People knew they were listening to the game, because they went up to them for score updates!

Never plan a wedding to conflict with an SEC football game. My daughter got married while the Razorbacks played Auburn out-of-state. (We call them **away games**.) But when game time ended up conflicting with the reception festivities, Daddy Don made sure the game was on at a special area at the reception. We had Razorback decorations, too. Several guests totally missed the harpist playing at the pergola, but that's all right.

Tailgating location is determined by early morning claims in some areas, and often by price. Our friends Debbie and Steve pay dearly to have an awesome spot, and open up their love of the Razorbacks to friends.

Nothing is better than the SEC and the fans who support these teams. It's as if the fans' effort in cheering on our teams gives them a true place on the team. But we have our rival teams. We only back a rival when it's SEC vs. anyone else.

When these phrases make sense to you, you know you're from the South:

Wooo Pig Sooie
Hotty Toddy
Hail State
Roll Tide
War Eagle
Or, Hook 'em Horns.

Horse Racing

Goin' to the races is one of my favorite springtime activities. I'm more of a people watcher, but sometimes my bets pay off. Don often encourages me to just "root" for a horse. It makes him crazy that I don't have a system, yet occasionally win.

My guys put a lot of time into trying to guess the horses — owner, past races, jockey, odds, weight, etc. They buy tip sheets and study them. Me? I pick a horse because I like the name, or the color. And you know what? I also like to bet the favored horse to place. I don't win much money, but I get to cash a ticket, so it makes it more fun. The way they bet and the way I do, the chance of winning is about the same.

My granddaddy liked to go to the Maryland trotter races. He built a spinner on the lid of a peanut can. A lot of people asked my Grampa Toby to spin for them!

The Derby, as in Churchill Downs, y'all, is big time. With mint juleps and lovely hats and those fascinators (the smaller hats that look like decorative headbands).

Even at the Arkansas Derby, I love to see bowties and seersucker.

According to Draper James (that's our belle Reese Witherspoon's clothing line), "Being well-dressed is a beautiful form of politeness."

Remember to wear shoes comfortable enough to keep on ALL day.... there's always a lot of walking on Derby Day.

The Garden Club

Every fine Southern woman likes to play in the dirt. We are proud of our flowers. Spring means getting everything trimmed back and ready, planting the stack of pots, and planting strawberries and tomatoes.

Remembering to wear gloves is difficult for me. I go outside in the morning to feed the dogs and occasionally am caught by my husband pulling weeds in my white cotton nightgown.

I have been known to run to the nursery with my gardening clothes on and dirty knees. Like Ouiser on *Steel Magnolias*, we all get a little eccentric as we age.

Some beloved Southern plants include: gardenias, dogwoods, camellias, crepe myrtles (I've heard them called, "summer's confetti"), magnolia trees, live oaks, azaleas, redbuds, muscadines, hydrangeas, climbing roses, Confederate jasmine, and paw-paw (May apple) trees. What did I miss?

My favorite flowers are tulips, daffodils, and pansies. And I love boxwoods. They serve as wonderful boundaries for types of gardens, and many of mine have arches and gates. My yard is filled with "garden rooms", including one made of stones, one just for cutting flowers, and my pebble-path herb garden. I have a Japanese arched bridge, two iron gazebos and a wooden peaked pergola that served as the dance floor at Natalie's wedding reception. One of the places I find peace is working in my yard — planting, trimming, watering, raking and waving at passers-by. That's a perfect time to pray, too.

Being a master gardener is on my bucket list.

I love to pass by an **ol' home place** (where a home once stood) and see a lone azalea bush or a clump of ancient daffodils.

Monograms

Even Elvis Presley loved monograms. He put TCB (Taking Care of Business) on everything.

The Greeks and Romans made coins with their monograms, so we just continue their tradition.

Seriously, we love our children's clothes, the pillows on our couches, our bedding, and our silver to be monogrammed. Pretty much anything can be monogrammed — your luggage, your beach towel, your ball cap, and your Yeti tumbler— even the back window of your car. One of my most prized possessions is a pewter tea set with our monogram that I bought on a trip to Colonial Williamsburg. I also love to find antique sterling flatware with original initials and monograms.

The Junior League

These ladies know how to cook. Purchase the local Junior League cookbook wherever you travel, and you'll have some of the best recipes ever.

Junior Leagues are not uppity white women doing good in the poor areas. They are educated women doing good for everyone. They're not all sitting around waiting for the "South to Rise Again." But, I did love that scene from *Something to Talk About* with Julia Roberts.

Southern Living Magazine

From gardening tips to house plans to decorating trends to the best new Southern food, every girl from Dixie knows this is the magazine to peruse. Garden and Gun is getting a big following. Because, gardening... and guns. But Don says he's never worn a tie on a hunt, nor does he intend to.

The Beauty Parlor

Nowadays we call it the salon, but whatever you call it, your ~~beautician~~ stylist is your confidant. A lot goes on at the beauty shop. A lot of gossip combined with a lot of love. My hairdresser is in charge of locating any new hairs that appear on my face. Like I said, Sandy's my friend.

Example: Truvy Jones in *Steel Magnolias*.

She also said, "Sweet tea is the house wine of the South."

Beauty Pageants

Most Southern girls have been "Miss Something," whether a pageant queen or princess, rodeo queen, or the homecoming queen. It may have been by choice or by force.

Beauty pageants are part of our Southern lifestyle. They teach poise and help young girls to perfect a talent. I've met our Miss Arkansas at one event or another over the last several years. Each Miss Arkansas is always kind and intelligent and lovely. She's always talented, too. Have you noticed that 9 times out of 10 a Southern girl wins Miss America? Take note.

Back in the day I won the local Junior Miss Pageant in high school. It was a "scholarship" pageant, so grades were involved. I danced for my talent, and met some nice girls, but..... Hmmm. Sorry. Not my thing. I see too many families who cannot afford the dresses, lodging, and transportation who really put themselves out on a limb for pageants. I guess it's their hobby.

I much prefer attending plays. I also enjoy dinner and a movie over going to casinos. To each his own.

Many years back I hosted a few "Miss America Parties" and they were quite entertaining. Guests selected a number upon arrival and were given a "state contestant". We had competition for the best dessert and appetizer and while we ate, we pretty much obliterated the contestants. We were heartless and hilarious. We crowned a winner and she always dressed up the next year.

We ladies are also pretty cruel while watching *The Bachelor*. But we love it. Women who go on there have no shame.

Surely there's a better way to find someone to share your "journey."

But we show true compassion while watching figure skating competition. Those ladies are athletes, and we hold our breath for their success.

Debutantes & Cotillion

I wish my daughter and I could have been debutantes, but we live in a town too small for that. Natalie did serve as personal assistant to the First Lady of Arkansas for a couple of years, so I believe her comportment is not in question.

I love that cotillion teaches young men to dance and how to properly treat young ladies. They learn how to wear a suit comfortably. Most girls love the opportunity to dress up.

Taylor told me when he was young, that he was not going to church as an adult, because he did not like "dressy clothes". I told him he'd just have to find a casual church then. However, when he was interviewing for jobs during his senior year of college, he asked me specifically to go with him to buy suits and sports jackets. A proud moment, for sure.

The closest thing these days to Finishing School is Cotillion. Your child will learn deportment, poise and manners. Money well spent.

But Southern mamas know that these lessons are best begun early, and at home.

Hunting and other Southern Pastimes

Dove hunting and Labor Day signal the end of summer. It still may be 80 degrees in October, but summer is over. Opening morning is all about friendship, good old-fashioned ribbing, and an excellent breakfast afterwards.

The opening day of **deer season** is sacred. When my husband was growing up they let school out that day. I heard about a girl who skipped class that day in college, because she thought it was a national holiday.

Even in my son's teenaged years, the opening night of **frog giggin'** usurped all girlfriends and dates. It was a guy thing.

We don't believe guns kill people. Guns are part of our culture. Crazy people use guns to kill, but any good Southerner has a few for each type of hunting (shotguns for bird hunting, rifles for deer and such) and maybe a couple for protection. It's not unusual for Southern fundraisers to include a gun raffle, and they usually bring in a lot of money.

Hunting is about food gathering and bragging rights.

And Southerners are not so concerned about pests like a squirrel in the attic. Troublesome pests often just get shot or poisoned. We're not like Yankees who call in pest control to remove the meddlesome animal.

"Hog killing weather" is when it finally cools off.

Taxidermy
Yes, our game room upstairs is full of mounts. All of them are trophies and there is a varied collection. My husband threatens to hang a deer head above our hearth downstairs, but hasn't yet.

Gun Safes
When Don finally bought one he wanted to put it in our foyer. Yes, downstairs by our front door. There was no way I'd agree to that. It's upstairs in the game room, and needless to stay I stayed out of the way the day they struggled to get it up there.

Kids learn to hunt by about age 8 if they are interested. They are required to take a hunter education class. Small town newspapers are filled with photos of children and their first bucks, or adults with a big trophy. And they smear deer blood on the child's face the first kill. This is similar to cutting the tail off of the shirt when a pilot completes his first solo flight.

The **"camp"** part of hunting is important. It's a male bonding time, with lots of cooking and card playing, and now with satellite TV, lots of football games. A man swears that at "camp" sleep is deeper and the food tastes better.

212

There are plenty of animals for hunting, with preservation programs enforced by Game & Fish, and we have good management programs. People from non-hunting families have become more accepting of the hunting lifestyle now that Farm-to-Table and organic meats have gained popularity. It is not about slaughter.

If you've ever eaten deer steak and gravy, bacon-wrapped jalapeño grilled doves, or duck & rice casserole you know what I mean. My husband gets the best jalapeño & cheese summer sausage made with his deer meat.

Taylor got chicken pox when he was in kindergarten. I was busy with Christmas season at my store. Don was duck hunting everyday, so he began taking Taylor with him as he began recovering. About the third day Tay announced that he was not going back and just planned to hang out with his daddy and go hunting every morning. Kindergarten dropout, I think not, but killing a limit in the flooded green timber is a powerful thing.

Why is it that a man can spot a deer from 200 yards, but cannot find the ketchup in the refrigerator?

Catfish is a true Southern fish.

Have you heard of noodlin'?

Cane pole fishin' just evokes a quiet day on the bank.

Runnin' trotline is a good pastime.

And we can immediately tell where someone is from by how they say Crappie and Bream.

There's nothing quite like a fish fry. The men normally fill up as they're cooking. And there's no better place to drain the grease than by dumping the fish fillets first into a paper towel-lined empty beer flat.

And we all know Christmas trees can best be recycled at the bottom of a pond.

Bass fishing — yes, we have huge tournaments in the South. These fishermen are revered for their fishing ability, and rewarded well, too.

Deep sea fishing — no beach vacay is complete without a run out into the gulf

When it snows you'll see a lot of camo. It's the only cold-weather clothing some people own, so it's a totally acceptable type of outerwear. As for hunting attire, good ol' boys tend to mock men who get outfitted head to toe from Orvis before their first hunting experience. Bass Pro Shop and Cabela's are perfectly acceptable sporting goods stores for building a wardrobe, however.

"Jingle bells and shotgun shells" describes Christmas decor in many man caves and camps during the holidays.

WWE — wraslin' (Wrestling)

NASCAR

Daytona International Speedway, Florida

Darlington Raceway, South Caroline

Talladega Superspeedway, Alabama

I have an acquaintance whose husband is an executive and did some work for Talladega. They were invited to sit in the box. Their tickets actually said, "no halter tops in box seating."

Rodeos, mud-ridin' & monster trucks are all a part of Southern Culture.

Note to Southern women:

Never throw out one of your man's baseball caps nor an old ice chest. These are extremely important to them, so leave them be.

Huntin' Dogs and Family Dogs

Never be jealous of a Southern guy's dog. He's had a dog by his side all his life, and it has taught him what a loyal companion is. He has lived through the pain of losing a beloved dog and he knows the loving face he can see every time he walks through the door.

We currently have four dogs. Don takes our Boykin Spaniel, "Junie B," to the farm with him everyday, which is a good thing because she likes to chew up everything... furniture, knitting projects, and pillows. She's adorable, but she wears me out. Don needs her to keep him company on his long days in the truck on the farm.

Bird dogs are my favorite. I love the faces of spaniels. But I've come to love mutts. They just want to be loved.

"Go awn 'n giiiiit" is an acceptable phrase in training a dog.

I love the joke:

Put your wife and your dog in the trunk of your car. Guess which one will be happy to see you when you **pop the trunk?**

Southerners love all types of dogs, but beware of a guy who loves a "purse dog." That's just weird.

Holiday Celebrations

<u>Thanksgiving</u>

Thanksgiving in the South is all about hunting and football as well as the meal and fellowship. I have found it to be a pretty old-fashioned holiday. Women cook, although the men will occasionally stand around in a group and fry a turkey. Our recipes form the traditions that make Southern Thanksgiving a wonderful holiday.

We give the blessing, offering thanks for family and praying for those in need. The men hunt before the meal, and often late afternoon, too. Football plays an important role in the day's entertainment... and before you know it everyone's peeking under the foil to see if it's time for leftovers.

I have wonderful memories of standing in front of the TV watching the Macy's Thanksgiving Day Parade, and twirling my baton, all by myself, in the middle of our living room. This was always on Thanksgiving morning, while my mother was slaving away in the kitchen.

National news shows always have segments about how to eat healthy over the holidays? Are they for real? We don't want to hear about that. If you're too full for dessert or choose not to have seconds that's your choice, but don't ask us to cut back on the butter, brown sugar, cream of something or another soup, or cream cheese in any of our Southern recipes.

We don't eat stuffing in the South. We leave the cavity of the bird alone and concentrate instead on creating dressing.

Sometimes dressing has chicken in it, but for Thanksgiving it is all about the cornbread and seasoned goodness in a pan of dressing. My mother-in-law makes exceptionally good dressing. She acts like it is simple, but I know she works on it for days. Every year we talk about having a "dressing day" so she can teach us how to make it. Some folks add oysters to the dressing.

Let us give thanks for Sister Schubert's rolls. Mini turkey sammies with mayonnaise are my favorite part of t-giving round two. Whether it's pumpkin pie or sweet potato pie, "cream" potatoes or mac and cheese, just make sure you have turkey and all the fixin's to feed your bunch.

Christmas vs. Thanksgiving

Retail — decorations are out early to jump-start sales
Real life — decorations go up after Thanksgiving
The "olden days" — a live tree was decorated Christmas Eve and remained until Epiphany. You've heard the song, The Twelve Days of Christmas. Well, it begins on December 25 with the celebration of Christ's birth and continues through January 6, Epiphany (sometimes called Three Kings' Day). This refers to the span of time between the birth of Christ and the coming of the Magi.

I wore myself and my staff out decorating for Christmas at the Periwinkle Place. One year we had thirteen trees. Bless their hearts.

At home, I leave my tree and decorations up until at least January 2nd. The week after Christmas is a quiet time of reflection and gratitude for me. I listen to Christmas carols and seasonal music and keep the spirit going. Prior to Christmas is so hectic.

Some crazy people have a different understanding of the meaning of the season. Some take their decorations down Christmas afternoon and throw their tree in the backyard. While others leave their artificial tree decorated and stuff it in an extra bedroom. Some folks begin decorating just after Halloween to enjoy their many decorations. That's just too early for me... and I like my autumn decor for Thanksgiving. But I completely understand.

I laugh when I see folks with pumpkins rotting on their porches in January. They apparently never use their front doors. I was shocked several years ago in Cleveland, Ohio, to see homes with Christmas decorations still intact in February. I guess they were frozen on and it was too difficult to remove them with all the snow and ice. Although, I have heard people joke about folks down South who leave lights up year-round on their homes.

Please refrain from putting colored lights on the exterior of your home. White lights represent purity and gentility. That's not to say I don't enjoy driving to see extreme light displays. But you'll never see colorful lights on my home.

And you did know that seeing colorful curtains from a home's exterior is a no-no? Use white linings or wooden shutters, but no turquoise curtains blazing from the street, please.

How to Enjoy Christmas

Buy gifts, lots of gifts, and give them to whomever you'd like. Don't let anyone tell you whom you must buy for. Just as the Three Wise Men brought gifts of love to the Baby Jesus, give to those you love.

Always have a "guest present" if someone a little unexpected comes to see you at Christmastime.

And slow down. Listen to holiday music, and sing along. Watch those Hallmark Christmas movies for two hours just for the kiss at the end. Shoot down some mistletoe from a tree and share it with a friend. Drive around to look at the Christmas lights. Bake and deliver to friends, family, your loved ones, a women's shelter, and whoever else you can.

Visit people who are important to you.

Drink hot cocoa with marshmallows AND whipped cream! And make all of your favorite foods. 'Tis the season.

Christmas Cards

I love sending and receiving Christmas cards. Whether they include a photo or not, I look through them several times, save a few, and enjoy the friendships I hold dearly.

But as a public service announcement, let's please leave the apostrophe out this year. It is the Browns, NOT the Brown's. If your name is Jones, add es, not ~~a high comma~~ an apostrophe. Just sayin'. Plural and possessive are different things. Makes me crazy and I wonder how you ever got that college degree.

Easter

I love the big crowd at church on Easter morning. I love the hymns, the promise of new beginnings, the flowers blooming outside, and all the festive clothes. I wish people treated every Sunday like Easter Sunday.

The sweetest sound in the world is hearing your grandchild tell the story of Christ's death and resurrection.

Again, the meal after Church is important in the South. Whether we go out or entertain family at home, a special menu and table setting is part of our holiday traditions.

Easter baskets are not just for children. When my children got "too big" for Easter, money started appearing in the eggs. Taylor was too cool to even carry a basket, but he wore roomy cargo shorts. The competition increased and became more cutthroat over time. My son-in-law wasn't invited to participate until he and Natalie were engaged!

With my grandbabies getting older, the traditions have reverted back to them. But I'm thinking about having an adult nighttime hunt next year with glow sticks in plastic eggs.

Living in an agricultural area, it has gotten quite popular for ag planes to drop eggs onto the field for children's hunts. It's pretty awesome to witness and will make you tear up just a little.

Vehicles and What-Not

Pickup trucks are a Southern staple.

White/Cream SUVs seem to be the South's "Mom Car."

Southern children typically learn to drive at an early age...whether they start out on a "4-wheeler" or their granddaddy's old Jeep, anytime after age nine is a reasonable age to see a child out on a country road. This is a throwback to the years children truly helped with harvest.

Hardship licenses are fairly common in the South. It allows kids to drive to school or an after-school job when they are as young as age 14. My children were disappointed to learn it wasn't a hardship for us to take them places, so they had to wait until age 16.

And by the way, we Southerners **crank** the car (start the engine).

Now that I'm older, I use the heat element in the seat more for back pain relief than for warmth!

Clean your **"ride"** before dates, weddings, and church. It's tough in the rural South to keep a vehicle clean. It's especially difficult in the Delta, where the bugs hitting the windshield at night sound like raindrops. (I learned a damp dryer sheet helps loosen the insects prior to washing.)

Tag — license plate. "He's got expired tags."

Glove box — glove compartment

Carry —"Can you carry me home" refers to getting a ride, not being lifted and carried.

Crack the window doesn't mean break it.

And not because I'm incapable, but if you live in the rural South a woman will never have need to change a tire. Farmers, gentlemen, and any good Southern guy will come to your rescue. And let them, because why not help them feel good about themselves? My husband has stopped to help people dozens of times. It's just what we do down South. When you inadvertently run into a ditch, you'll be lucky to see a group of guys pile out of a pick-up truck to help pull your vehicle out.

Road Trips

We live in such a small town. When my children were little they would often ask, "Where are we?" And, as we were most often between towns I would just answer them, "In the middle of nowhere." That didn't mean it wasn't scenic or lacked value, I just couldn't name a town because we weren't there yet.

Now, for big city Southerners, you can drive and drive and still be in the same city. ~~Bad~~ Good examples are Baton Rouge, Atlanta, and Houston. But for the rest of us, we measure distance in minutes. Since we don't have much rush hour traffic (except when a train stops the kids heading out to the high school campus) we just say it takes 30 minutes to get to the movie theater and an hour and a half to get to Little Rock. If you're late, being stuck behind a combine during harvest is a perfectly acceptable excuse.

We give a courtesy wave when a driver lets us enter in front of him. We acknowledge neighbors when we pass them and the street.

And, we don't honk at the person in front of us the second the light changes.

Roadkill is pretty prevalent in the South. These dead varmints give our visitors the chance to see armadillos, 'possums, and 'coons up close. It's sad to see deer and dogs on the side of the road. We all know Loudon Wainwright's song, "Dead Skunk in the Middle of the Road." (1972)

Littering is another pet peeve. I don't see a reason for it. It's just disrespectful to our country and to God's beautiful creation.

To **squall tires** is something all young boys wanna do. Does it need an explanation?

Doin' donuts is another teenage past time.

Hoopty cars are beater vehicles that are in poor and shabby condition. Sometimes the owners make sure they have nice rims. This is what Hollywood directors typically use when filming movies in the South. It's like they think the only car dealerships are in Los Angeles.

Twilla is a really good car dancer. She gently changes the direction of the car, and taps the brakes to the beat of whatever is on the radio. Her grandkids think she's super cool. I used to intentionally hit pockets of water. We called it waterskiing.

And if you're from up north, just because you can drive on snow and ice doesn't mean we can. Don't pick on us. We're just unprepared.

Wondering if its PC to yell "shotgun!" anymore when you want to sit up front?

Traveling

A Southern girl may travel more casually now than my mother used to (suit and gloves), but never in sweats or pajama pants. Air travel used to be a luxury. Now it is drudgery. But any self-respecting person dresses for his or her own comfort as well as to make others feel comfortable. You never know who you'll meet.

While on an airplane, be mindful of putting your seat back and making the person behind you uncomfortable. The seats only recline about three inches now, so you might as well stay put. If the person in front of you seems rudely unaware of crowding you, kindly bringing it to his/her attention can bring positive results. It's tough. We're uncomfortable, but kindness is key.

And please teach your little ones not to kick the seat!

And by the way, isn't Uber the most stupendous thing to come along?

Tipping isn't tricky. Just be generous, because the incomes of frontline people depend on you. Tip 15-20% when eating out. Same to tour guides when on a cruise ship excursion, etc. $5-$10 is good for a valet or bell person. I leave a bill at the end of a vacation stay for the cleaning person. Tip at Sonic. They have to work outside.

It is not necessary to tip for a carryout meal. Oftentimes the computer asks if you'd like to add a tip. That person is paid hourly, and not receiving a waitress's salary, so there's no need to feel guilty.

It was nice to see folks add a little tip, though, during all the curbside service of Covid-19.

Using a Concierge

The concierge can answer your questions about sites and attractions, make meal reservations, and order your tickets to plays and concerts. Tip this person and don't be intimidated to ask for their services. The concierge is provided to make your stay more efficient and pleasant.

And please don't say, "conseridge."

Gift Giving

We Southern girls like to give gifts. We like to receive gifts. It's all about feeling special. Giving a gift is both personal and meaningful, and an investment of your time.

When I had my gift shop, those of us who worked together would occasionally leave little gifts for one another. We always signed the card, "Love, your PPSP." Of course, we all knew each other's handwriting, but it was just fun getting a gift from your Periwinkle Place Secret Pal.

A "Little Happy" or a "Sussy" (surprise) is a gift you buy for a friend for no reason... like if you know your friend loves bunny rabbits and you found just the cutest little bunny paperweight for her desk.

Wonderful presentation adds to the anticipation.

We believe you should pause to appreciate a well-wrapped gift. The wrapping on a gift can be as important as the gift itself. Twilla, lives by this standard. In fact, I know she could win a national gift-wrapping competition.

A surcée is another word for a "just because" gift. It's unexpected, and often used to refer to "a little something tied on top." At the Periwinkle Place, the first surcée was born when we accidentally left an item out of a gift box so we tied it in cellophane on the outside of the gift. Before long, customers began requesting this because it improved the presentation!

I've always found buying gifts to be easy. When I see something I like I think of who else it will appeal to. I have to keep lists of what I've bought. Some people are just easier than others to buy for.

I once had a customer who joked that Christmas was getting expensive. Every gift she bought she loved so much that she had to buy another — for herself!

How to be a Fun Grandmother

Let them jump on the bed.

Make up silly songs and sing them every time you are together. The "back it up" song taught my grandtwins how to manage climbing up and down stairs.

Draw pictures and let them guess what it is (My children's Granny is excellent at this game!)

Let them help in the kitchen.

Let them eat popsicles in the bathtub, and play with Play-Doh outside.

Read to them until they cannot hold their eyes open. I like to substitute the wrong words when we read a story they have heard a million times. I love to hear their laughter when I trick them.

Pretend that you cannot pronounce hippopotamus.

Encourage them to get muddy or dirty.

Let them take huge bubble baths and let them stay in as long as they'd like. After all, you don't have the kind of schedule their parents have. And remember, you'll have plenty of time to clean up after they've gone home.

Pretend you're in a restaurant and "take their order" before making lunch or a snack. They'll eat better if you do this, so that's a plus.

Teach your grandchildren to pump their arms at truck drivers so they'll toot their semi's horn.

Southern grandparents often have unique names.... Besides grandma and grandpa. Honey, Shug, Grammy, Ga Ga, Sweet Mama, Mimi, DeDe, GiGi and my name is MeMommy. My father-in-law, the kindest man to ever grace this earth, was called PeePaw.

Grandparents should feel free to help teach their grandchildren how to whistle, skip a stone, wink, snap their fingers, draw a heart and star, blow bubblegum bubbles, tie a shoe, compliment others, and pick up trash.

I love older Southern ladies. They can say whatever they want to say, and people excuse them. They whisper too loudly from the back pew. They will let you know when you've put on a little weight. And they'll pray for your family, and ask about your mama, and they'll love you. We revere them for their quirks and for what they did to get us to where we are today.

Thanks for Readin', y'all.

Don and I once broke in line at the funeral home. We sneaked in the back way to share our condolences with the family. We simply could not wait in line because Don had a meeting he was in charge of. I know this wasn't right; especially because there were **thirty-eleven** people in line.

My suggestion to you is:

We all break etiquette rules! Do it with a laugh, and make sure mama isn't watching.

To be totally honest, I have one faux pas for which I am truly ashamed. I could have avoided it if I had had less wine to drink and had I not shared the situation with my best friend and daughter. Once, at a wedding, I turned to Twilla and said, "Oops, I just threw up in my mouth a little bit." She likes to remind me of this occasionally. Well, often.

I've also wet my pants in public from laughter, more than twice.

Just try, people.

Made in the USA
Monee, IL
09 May 2021